DYSON'S DELIGHT

DYSON'S DELIGHT

An anthology of
SIR GEORGE DYSON'S
writings and talks
on music

selected, edited and introduced
by
CHRISTOPHER PALMER

Thames Publishing
London

For
Alice and Freeman
in memory of their father

ISBN 0 905210 48 4

Text © 1989 Alice Dyson
Introduction © 1989 Christopher Palmer

We are grateful to the editors of the journals
in which these articles originally appeared
for permission to reprint

Printed by Hobbs the Printers of Southampton

Contents

Sir George Dyson, c.1959

Introduction

(i)

In January 1957, Herbert Howells wrote to Sir George Dyson – then living in retirement in Winchester – to tell him that he was assembling a collection of clavichord pieces to be entitled *Howells' Clavichord*, each dedicated to a friend and contemporary of the composer. Howells proposed so to favour Dyson, and to call his piece 'Dyson's Delight'. In due course the album appeared, and the letter in which Dyson expressed his 'delight' to Howells is reproduced in facsimile on p. 105.

It was a good title, so fitting that I have had no scruple in appropriating it for the present collection. Delight was the keynote in Dyson's life. He enjoyed his world and his work, and communicated that enjoyment in every word and note he wrote. He had good reason, since for the most part fate dealt kindly with him. His parents were working-class but exerted themselves to the utmost that he should fulfil his early promise – which he more than did. At the Royal College of Music he established an excellent rapport not only with Parry but also – and this was no mean achievement – with Stanford, his composition teacher: the foundations for his later composing career being thereby set sure. He emerged relatively unscathed from the Great War: he was invalided home suffering from shell-shock before he could sustain any greater injury or lose his life. In fact his Manual of Grenade-Fighting – officially adopted by the War Office – sold so well that he made a tidy sum of money (it was typical of the man that whatever circumstances forced him into doing he did well, even if it was killing Germans). He was happily married for over 40 years; his two children turned out a credit to him in their different ways;[1] and his multi-divided career as schoolmaster, broadcaster, lecturer, author, administrator, performing/practical

---

1. Alice became an almoner, Freeman a world-famous physicist; grandson George is the author of *Baidarka*, the story of the author's discovery and reconstruction of the Alaskan portable boat and how he travelled far and wide in it.

musician and composer flourished exceedingly. There were no set-backs, no disasters, no major disappointments: even at the end he was lucky, for he suffered neither incapacitating illness nor the loss of his partner (his wife, though older, outlived him by more than 10 years). In old age he looked back on a life of distinguished achievement in many fields, and died in September 1964 a happy man.

His music reflects this happiness. 'A nice old stick — always had a twinkle in his eye.' Thus composer Laurie Johnson, who was a student at the RCM mid-way through Dyson's directorate. There are plenty of 'twinkles' in his music, and not merely in *The Canterbury Pilgrims*. *All* his music registers a relish. Sir Keith Falkner once described him as a 'liberal Conservative' in music as in life.[2] Certainly the sense of a living English tradition is strong. Think of Parry with his feeling for English poetry, for vocal colour and texture, for broad and sonorous climaxes; remember Stanford's keen dramatic and descriptive sense, his greater depth of feeling for orchestral colour, for the effectiveness of unexpected key-shifts. Now complement these qualities with something of Strauss's orchestral panache, Delius's poetic colour-harmony (with its more sophisticated, aristocratic demeanour) and consistent warmth of lyrical, even romantic expression: and you have something approaching the Dyson idiom. No more Elgar than what is already endemic in Parry; some trace of Vaughan Williams, but not much (it is extraordinary, incidentally, to listen to the early *Three Rhapsodies* for string quartet and discover this most comfortably English of all composers speaking with so accomplished a German accent as to cast doubts on his being English at all! No sound of a foreign tongue remains in later years. All the vital nutrients are conspicuously well absorbed). Not a markedly original idiom, as Dyson himself admits; but no-one has to be original to be interesting. Dyson's is above all very *musical* music, exquisitely made (one would expect nothing less than first-rate craftsmanship from a pupil of Stanford), grateful to perform and to listen to, tonic in effect. We feel the better for having listened;

---

2. In his review of my Dyson monograph (*Musical Times*, October 1986, p. 625), Stephen Banfield commented that my chapter on Dyson the man 'reminds us how distant a musical society based on paternal liberalism has become for most of us, and perhaps how much we may have lost with its passing ...'

we are filled with that sense of well-being which only music that sings and sounds fit and well, and which makes a point of sounding beautiful, can give us.

(ii)

Dyson's characteristically un-self-revealing autobiographical sketch (see p. 25) needs some enlarging upon, although readers will find a fairly detailed account of his life in my *George Dyson – a Centenary Appreciation* (London 1984). Dyson does not say that he came from a working-class background. His father was a blacksmith, his mother a weaver. He celebrated his father's profession in the most unconventional of his choral works, *The Blacksmiths*, a virtuoso setting of a mediaeval alliterative poem in Middle English. Here it is in its original form:

> Swarte smekyd smethes smatyred wyth smoke
> Dryve me to deth wyth den of here dyntes.
> Such noys on nyghtes ne herd men never:
> What navene cry and clateryng of knockes!
> The cammede kongons cryen after 'col, col!'
> And blowen here bellewes, that al here brayn breasts
> 'Huf, puf!', saith that on; 'haf, paf!' that other.
> Thei spitten and spraulyn and spellyn many spelles;
> Thei graven and gnacchen, thei groanys togydyr,
> And holden hem hote wyth here hard hamers.
> Of a bole-hyde ben here barm-fellys;
> Here shankes ben shakeled for the fere flunders;
> Heavy hamerys thei han, that hard ben handled,
> Stark strokes thei stryken on a stelyd stokke:
> Lus, bus! las, das! rowtyn be rowe.
> Swech doleful a dreme the devyl it todryve!
> The mayster longith a litel, and lascheth a lesse,
> Twineth hem tweyn, and toucheth a treble:
> Tik tak! hic hac! tiket taket! tyk, tak!
> Lus bus, las das! such lyfe they ledyn
> Alle clothermerys: Cryst hem gyve sorwe!
> May no man for brenwaterys on night han hys rest!

This is the freely adapted and modernised version which Dyson set to music, almost certainly the work of his wife Mildred:

9

Swart, smirched smiths, smattered with smoke
Drive me to death with din of their dents.
Such noise on nights ne'er heard men never;
Such clashing of cries and clattering of knocks.
The craftsman clamour for 'Coal, coal, coal!',
And blow their bellows, their brains to burst.
They jostle and jangle, they jape and they jest,
They groove and they grind, they grumble together,
Hot with the heaving of heated hammers.
Of thick bull's-hide are their branded aprons;
Their shanks are shod 'gainst shooting sparks.
Huge hammers they have, and hard to handle;
Stark strokes strike they on the steeléd stock.
'Well wrought! Well wrought! Well wrought!'
Might daunt the devil, such life they lead
All armourers, founders, forgemen –
                                    Christ them save!

The Canterbury Pilgrims is partially dedicated 'to M.L.D., who prepared the words', i.e., who modernised Chaucer for singing purposes. Her presence or influence is to be guessed-at in the literary aspect of many a Dyson choral opus: one instance merely of the many congenial elements that went to make up an 'abiding partnership' (*vide inf.*). That the mature Dyson retained no trace of self-consciousness about his background, and never became a snob (as people in his case often do), is mainly due, I imagine, to the ease with which Mildred Atkey made it possible for him to do the necessary social climbing.

Of his marriage and personal life Dyson says nothing whatever in the autobiographical chapter. He discussed it frankly in a letter to his son, however, when the latter was contemplating marriage:

I think that passion itself is fundamentally a blind mechanism, which may have very little to do with what I will call permanent affection; and this is why marriage is such a gamble, particularly for both of pronounced individuality. What matters in marriage is the day after day, year after year accumulation of trivial but common incidents, accidents, thoughts and mutual experiences that go to make a permanent background, not for passion, but for friendship. I am chary of an overwhelming and possessive attachment, because I think most of that is just a biological urge like eating and drinking which may exhaust itself at the expense of its victims and leave nothing on which to build permanently. That is why the 'arranged' marriages of France seem to result, in most cases, in the extraordinarily close and private domesticity of the average French household. Two people who hardly know each other, as we should think, by virtue of belonging to two families which have a compatible status, social, cultural and financial, find in their time a domestic way of life which is both congenial and satisfying. I felt this quite strongly even as a very young man, and though I had many an attack of what I call 'passion', I always said to myself, 'steady marriage is a much more serious business than this. Don't let your instincts undermine your common sense.' And when finally at the age of 34 I married your Mamma there was little of romantic passion on my side, any more than there was on hers. I wanted someone who had a solid background of the kind I wanted to live in, day after day, forever. It was more of a gamble for Mamma because I had lived such a varied life and had only arrived at her class by climbing. But I am sure she counted too, on mutual friends, tastes and interests to cement us into an abiding partnership, and that is precisely what has happened. There are many more romantic attachments and temperaments, but I am certain there are few or none that are happier. Each of us has become an acquired taste, quite unbreakable; poor material for an autobiography or play, but extraordinarily satisfying to live with. When you are 66 I hope you feel as serene as I do...[3]

Dyson was one of those who, by a rare and winning combination of talent, personality and good fortune, seem able to make the world adapt itself to them. All through his life, either he made wise and happy choices for himself, or others made them for him. Even the war years were productive, at least in retrospect. In December 1955, by now retired and living in Winchester, Dyson sends a 32nd birthday greeting to his son and recalls:

...my own 32nd anniversary was spent on Salisbury Plain training hand-grenadiers, prior to going to France in 1915, and I did not come back to my own job for more than five years after that! ... Looking back on my own gap I would go to great lengths to avoid living it again, and yet it did in

---

3. This letter was written in 1949. Eight years later, at the time of the break-up of Freeman's first marriage, his father recapitulated much the same material. 'I was never "in love" with Mamma in the passionate sense, or she with me. I wanted someone who had the background, the connections, the attitude of mind, the social and intellectual commonsense that I could love and respect all day and everyday, with or without any deeper emotion. I had managed to climb into her class; your uncle Freeman and his and my friends were all part of it. And I wanted to fix myself there for good. We understood one another's speech, we had the same values, the frank give-and-take of genuine friendship, and a whole world of personal and intellectual tastes in common. We have now had 40 years of this unalloyed companionship, with never a doubt or disturbance of any kind.'

11

some ways act as a purgative. It knocked all the aesthetic cobwebs and preciosities out of one, and made the return to normal − if one survived − like being consciously born again, at the same time sensitive and mature. I am quite sure I should have been a far narrower product if I had not had that shattering ... I don't know why I am meandering like this at you. It is hardly a birthday poem. But I am sitting quietly in my little study upstairs, the sun is shining, the sky blue, the temperature mild, and my thoughts just wander over a long past.

After the war and his marriage came Winchester, the place he loved best in all England, where he spent the happiest years of his professional life, wrote some of his happiest music, and whither he returned in retirement to end his days. That Winchester is one of the loveliest English cities of ancient foundation scarcely needs saying; and in those days of no high-rise buildings and car-parks and far fewer cars its charm must have been even more potent. Then there was the College itself, embodying as it did precisely that tradition of civilised Englishness − 600 years of it − which was most precious to Dyson. He lived in two beautifully spacious houses − first in Kingsgate Street, then St Swithun Street − both highly congenial to his life-style as it had evolved: on the one hand teaching, conducting, organ-playing, writing, lecturing, broadcasting, composing; on the other bringing up his two small children. In October 1957 he wrote to Freeman:

> ... the most creative work I have ever done − *The Canterbury Pilgrims* and two very successful books − were produced when I was at my busiest with other jobs ... there was a period when I was doing a weekly broadcast, lecturing between trains in Edinburgh and Glasgow, conducting my various societies among my chapel services and teaching, and at the same time contriving to write both music and prose as good as or better than at any other time in my life. As I look back on it, I just wonder how on earth I managed to be so active and fertile, but I am quite sure that the sheer quantity and variety of my jobs stimulated me as no isolated brain-pushing would have done ...

James Sabben-Clare, the present Headmaster of Winchester College, notes that when Dyson was appointed to the staff in 1924 it was at the very top of the salary scale, nearly £1,000 (a princely sum in those days, particularly for a teacher). 'George Dyson was a dapper, trim figure; with his bow-tie, stubby moustache and centre parting he looked like a senior staff officer. Like many small men he had enormous energy. This enabled him to combine his College work with a multitude of outside commitments ... not that the school suffered from this diversification. The moribund orchestra was resuscitated, and the members of the Glee Club rose to an all-time peak of 176. Choral and organ scholarships to Oxford and Cambridge were won for the first time. In 1936 he helped to bring about the biggest improvement of all: the Quiristers were released from their ages-old sentence of menial servitude in the college hall. With this social incubus removed they could be properly selected, educated and trained in music ...'[4] One other innovation which left a permanent mark was the founding of the Winchester Music Club, whose first conductor Dyson was. By the time he left in 1937 to take over the directorship of the Royal College of Music, he had achieved such a spread of musical activity that nearly 40% of the school took part as players or singers in the termly concerts. The Dyson obituary in the *Wykehamist* (3 November 1964) commented more generally that 'he liked other people, whether high or low, and he liked the scholastic climate of Winchester. He could keep the clever boy at full stretch, and could also coax and charm a choir to excel itself. His relationships with others as teacher, administrator and conductor, were of the happiest'. It is possible that the enduring freshness of Dyson's music is due at least in part to his humanizing contact with children and young people and his sympathy with them.

Dyson was a man who always relished a challenge, and his RCM years (1937–1951) taxed his ability in a way he could only have foreseen dimly, if at all. A vivid picture of the college at war is painted by Freeman Dyson in his *Disturbing the Universe*:

My father's finest hour came at the same time as England's, at the beginning of the Second World War. He was then no longer a school-teacher. He had moved to London to be director of the Royal College of Music, one of the two major musical conservatories of England. When the war and the bombing of London began, the government and his own board of trustees urged him to evacuate the college to some safe place in the country. He refused to budge. He pointed out to the trustees that his college provided a livelihood to at least half of the leading orchestral players and artists in London. Most of these people came to the college to teach two or three days a week and could not live on concerts alone. If the college were evacuated,

4. *Winchester College* (Southampton 1981), pp. 120–122.

13

one of two consequences would follow. Either the college would lose its best teachers, or the musical life of London would be effectively closed down for the duration of the war. And in either case the careers of a whole generation of musicians would be ruined. So my father had one of the offices in the college converted into a bedroom and announced that he would stay there to keep the place running so long as any roof remained over his head. His board of trustees accepted his decision and the college stayed open. Hearing of this, the other big London conservatory, which had already made plans to evacuate, changed its mind and stayed open too. London remained musically alive, nourishing fresh talents and giving them a chance to be heard, through the six years of war. My father stayed steadfast at his post at the college, helping to put out fires on the roof at night and conducting student orchestras during the day. The only substantial loss that the college sustained was a little opera theatre with an irreplaceable collection of antique operatic costumes. The damage was done at night when the professors and students were out of the building. Nobody, from the beginning of the war to the end, was injured on the premises.

During the war years I often went to lunch with my father and the professors in the college dining room. These people were hardboiled professional musicians, averse to any display of sentiment. Their conversation consisted mainly of professional gossip and jokes. But I could feel the warmth of their loyalty to the college and the sense of comradeship that bound them and my father together. The daily experience of shared hardships and dangers created a spirit of solidarity in the college which people who have known academic institutions only in times of peace can hardly imagine. I was reminded of this spirit when I watched the citizens of bombed-out Münster perform their open-air opera in 1947, and when I heard my American friends tell tales of wartime Los Alamos.

I ate one memorable lunch at the College at the height of the V-1 bombardment in the summer of 1944. My father and his professors were talking merrily about their plans for the expansion of the college to take care of the flood of students that would be pouring in as soon as the war was over. From time to time there was a momentary break in the conversation when the putt-putt of an approaching V-1 could be heard in the distance. The talk and the jokes continued while the putt-putt-putt grew louder and louder until it seemed the beast must be directly overhead. Again there was a momentary break in the conversation when the putt-putt suddenly stopped, and the room was silent for the five seconds that it took the machine to descend to earth. Then an ear-splitting crash, and the conversation continued without a break until the next quiet putt-putt-putt could be heard in the distance. I was thinking lugubrious thoughts about the consequences that a direct hit on our dining room would have for the musical life of England. But such thoughts seemed to be far from the minds of my father and his colleagues. During the whole of our leisurely lunch, the subject of the V-1 bombardment was never once mentioned.

I used to talk a great deal to my father, especially during the early years of the war, about the morality of fighting and killing. At first I was a convinced pacifist and intended to become a conscientious objector. I agonized endlessly over the ethical line that had to be drawn between justifiable and unjustifiable participation in the war effort. My father listened patiently while I expounded my wavering principles and rationalised the latest shifts in my pacifist position. He said very little. My ethic doctrines grew more and more complicated as I was increasingly torn between my theoretical repudiation of national loyalties and my practical involvement in the life of a country fighting with considerable courage and good humour for its survival. For my father the issues were simple. He did not need to argue with me. He knew that actions speak louder than words. When he moved his bed into the college he made his position clear to everybody. When things were going badly in 1940, he said, 'All we have to do is to behave halfway decently, and we shall soon have the whole world on our side.' When he spoke of the whole world, he was probably thinking especially of the United States of America and of his own son.[5]

Malcolm Arnold has recently given us a warming reminiscence of Dyson as Director:

I was 17 when I first came to London. I was disappointed by my progress at the Royal College of Music in London, where I had a scholarship, so I ran away with a very beautiful Welsh art student with red hair from the Royal College of Art. I picked Plymouth because it was in Devon, and seemed to be a romantic place. We had a lovely time there, but I was glad to come back. In fact, I was invited back to the College. I had written a very rude letter to Sir George Dyson, the Principal, but in reply he wrote me a marvellous letter, asking me to come back. He was very much maligned because he had written an Army Manual on the hand grenade during the First War, and all us young people at the college did not value him as a musician or as a person because of that – but I did in later life. I thought he was a marvellous man. He was a great friend to me.[6]

Dyson's years of retirement (he resigned from the RCM in 1952 and he and Lady Dyson settled in Winchester among their old friends) were lit up and gladdened by a wonderful Indian summer as a composer. The years fell away as if they had never been, and in the fullness of maturity (with all its advantages in terms of efficiency and technical confidence) he produced work after work

5. London and New York 1979, pp. 85–7.
6. *Music and Musicians*, October 1986, pp. 8–9

of untarnished lyrical freshness, most of them about spring, youth, love and rebirth. Look merely at some of the titles: *Hierusalem, Sweet Thames run softly* (a setting of a shortened form of Spenser's *Prothalamion*)[7], *Let's go a-maying* (Herrick), *A Spring Garland, A Christmas Garland, A Summer Day.* The *Christmas Garland*, composed in 1959, was Dyson's last major work and has that lovely simplicity which only the finest workmanship can achieve. There are some fine anthems — *Live for ever, glorious Lord* and *Hail, Universal Lord* (Milton), both inflamed by the same ecstasy, joy-in-life; as are the *Three Rustic Songs* (Herrick) for men's voices and piano. On his own admission Dyson wrote only to please himself and his friends, none of whom were unduly enamoured of 'wrong notes'. Of his various works in progress he wrote to Freeman (May 8 1949) 'however much, or little, value they have ... it is my main recreation, needs no apparatus, and has no end.' The *Fantasia and Ground Bass* for organ is a fine work on a big scale, the only time Dyson really exerted himself creatively on behalf of an instrument he had played all his life. He continued to lecture, broadcast, chair committees, and conduct (particularly the *Pilgrims*) but with some falling-off of frequency as deafness began to be a problem (he noted to Freeman that *pianissimo* tended to become complete silence). He grew frail but was never seriously ill or affected mentally, and as the end approached was nursed comfortably at home; his daughter Alice, with her experience as a hospital almoner, saw to that. The last letters to Freeman are remarkably uncomplaining:

---

7. In March 1955, after the first performance of *Sweet Thames* at the Winchester Festival, Dyson wrote to Freeman: 'I think I really hit the nail on the head. It is to have several other performances quite soon, one of which I am broadcasting at the Malvern Festival in May. And the publishers have already had to reprint it! ...' Frank Howes in *The Times* (March 25 1955) wrote a notice that is a model of sympathetic discernment: 'Spenser's *Prothalamion* breathes a pastoral spirit of England in spring which Dyson caught with sure touch in his *Canterbury Pilgrims*. He has similar opportunities in his new cantata ... the two abiding strands in the English character, the simplicity of the country and the dignity of the town, find expression in a setting in which there is sufficient harmonic complexity, mostly in the orchestral part, to paint the fresh colours of the riverside, but consistently diatonic vocal lines, such as Parry knew how to write for English words, to suggest youth and sweetness. Indeed, if it were not for the reference to Spain, one would think that Elizabethan England had not a care in the world.'

... Mamma, who is some years older [than I], is in wonderfully active trim, and we do our 'Darby and Joan' routine quietly a day at a time ... I have made an abridged version of the *Canterbury Pilgrims* for female voices, probably my last effort in this line ... on the whole I have much to be thankful for. (March 8 1964)

Finally:

... I can go on from day to day quietly at home and help mildly with the chores, but I have no reserves of energy, and am not fit to stand and make speeches. Mamma is wonderful, shops and does all her household tasks, and is cheerful and ready. She is worth about three of me ... (April 6 1964)

(iii)

Dyson was not only a composer but also a writer, and was generally happiest when setting words to music. One of his keenest sources of delight throughout his life was literature, particularly poetry. Never a man to do anything by halves, Dyson's knowledge and understanding of poetry ranged way beyond that of the dedicated amateur. Early on in the war the BBC asked him for a patriotic hymn for massed singing, leaving the choice of text to him. He finally found a poem of Sir William Watson to which he needed to make some slight adjustments for technical reasons. To the BBC official who was handling the commission he explained that 'my small changes are in the main due to the importance of reconciling the *scansion* of the two verses. If the melody is to be both broad in style and grateful to sing, one must have equal numbers of syllables in the parallel lines of the two verses, and the main accents must also coincide ...' The poem's title, 'Motherland', was also Dyson's invention, and the letter well illustrates the totally professional thoroughness with which Dyson always approached the setting of words to music, whether on a small or large scale.[8] A letter to Freeman (January 20 1956) mentions the possibility of a book,

---

8. Dyson was no respecter of poems in their original form when it was a matter of meeting his musical needs. In 1958 he wrote *Hail, Universal Lord*, an anthem for St Matthew's Church, Northampton, 'words by John Milton'. The reader will search in vain for any poem of Milton bearing this title. The words are in fact a very skilful selection and rearrangement of lines from Book V of *Paradise Lost*.

17

a 'comparatively modest essay founded on some lectures about poetry that I gave at London University in 1946 and of which I have copious notes.' Alas, the book never materialised, and the 'copious notes' have failed to survive.

With few exceptions Dyson's choice of texts for setting to music was beyond reproach and often ventured into regions quite far removed from the normal course of those who read poetry. The latter could treat themselves to an hour or so of unlooked-for enjoyment merely by perusing the texts of Dyson's choral works, particularly the 'anthologies'. Take *Quo Vadis*, for example. Most of us know our Wordsworth (the Immortality Ode), our Sarum Psalter ('God be in my Head'), our Shelley ('The one remains, the many change and pass') and the hymns of Keble, one of Dyson's more questionable enthusiasms. But where should we be if asked about Barnaby Barnes, for example:

> O whither shall my troubled music incline,
> If not the glorious scaffold of the skies,
> Nor highest heaven's resplendent hierarchies,
> Where heavenly soldiers in pure armour shine ...

Then there is Thomas Sternhold, of Sternhold and Hopkins, versifiers of the Psalms:

> The Lord descended from above,
> And bowed the heavens on high,
> And underneath his feet he cast
> The darkness of the sky;
> On Cherubim and Seraphim
> Full royally he rode,
> And on the wings of mighty winds
> Came flying all abroad.

Now some unfamiliar Cardinal Newman, author of *The Dream of Gerontius*:

> They are at rest:
> We may not stir the heaven of their repose
> By rude invoking voice, or prayer addressed
>   In waywardness to those
> Who in the mountain grots of Eden lie,
> And hear the four-fold river as it murmurs by.

Herrick was a favourite. Your Herrick and mine is probably the poet of rosebuds ripe to be gathered, daffodils hasting away too soon, and of the silk-clad Julia.[9] Dyson knew the insomniac, waiting and watching for the morning:

Night hath no wings, to him that cannot sleep;
And time seems then, not for to fly, but creep;
Slowly her chariot drives, as if that she
Had broke her wheel.
So 'tis with me, who listening pray
The winds, to blow the tedious night away ...

Dyson found in Herrick a fellow-lover of London, and its river; for as the second of his *Three Rustic Songs* the former sets to music, to what is perhaps the most glorious melody he ever composed:

No more shall I along thy crystal glide,
In barge with boughs and rushes beautified;
Never again shall I with finny oar
Put from, or draw unto the faithful shore:
And landing here, or safely landing there,
Make way to my beloved Westminster ...

The *Christmas Garland* contains hardly a single familiar Christmas text. Instead:

Wake, O earth, wake everything!
Wake and hear the joy we bring;
Wake and joy; for all this night
Heaven and every twinkling light,
    All amazing
    Still stand gazing

---

9. When Dyson was a student he lived with relatives in Greenwich and used to cycle in each day to the Royal College. Had he known it he would have enjoyed the parody of one of Herrick's most famous lyrics which appeared in the *Cambridge Revue* in December 1896:

Whenas on wheels my Julia goes
Then, then methinks how sweetly shows
The pistol-action of her toes.

Next when I cast mine eyes and see
That brave vibration each way free
Oh how that waggling taketh me!

(printed in *Cambridge Commemorated – An Anthology of University Life* ed. Laurence and Helen Fowler, Cambridge 1984)

Angels, powers and all that be,
Wake, and joy this sun to see.

That was William Austin, (1587–1634), author of the 'Hymn
to a Musician' which Dyson set as No. 2 of his *Three Choral Hymns*.
Then (still in *A Christmas Garland*) we find Crashaw's

We saw thee in thy balmy nest,
Young dawn of our eternal day!
We saw thine eyes break from the East
And chase the trembling shades away.

An anonymous poet, in Dyson's second movement of the same work,
sings of

Sweet music, heavenly rare
Mine ears doth greet

– which is an apt enough description of *all* the music to which
the words of the cantata are set. Of course, Herrick is represented:

... Say, if this new birth of ours
Sleeps, laid within some ark of flowers,
Spangled with dew-light ...

– and this 'of course' – for Dyson set Herrick more frequently
than any other poet – prompts me to wonder about Walford
Davies's *Noble Numbers*, an oratorio written for the 1909 Three
Choir Festival at Hereford, and one of his finest works. The words
come for the most part from Herrick's eponymous collection of
poems on sacred subjects, together with contemporary poems
by George Herbert, Donne and anon; the point being that Dyson
also set 'Weigh me the fire' and 'In the hour of my distress' in
Quo Vadis; 'Yet if his majesty our sovereign Lord' (anon) in
A Christmas Garland; and Herbert's 'Let all the world in every
corner sing' in the *Three Songs of Praise*. The Sarum Prayer 'God
be in my Head', best known in Walford Davies's setting, also turns
up in *Quo Vadis*. Walford Davies was one of the first English
composers to apply the anthology-principle to oratorio, cantata
and song-cycle; his taste in poetry was generally sound;[10] and he

---

10. Eg, he set some marvellous Spenser in *High Heaven's King*, Alice Meynell in
Christ in the Universe, selections from the *Divine Comedy* in the *Fantasy* for

and Dyson were over many years united in friendship and mutual admiration. So it is reasonable to assume some degree of influence, whether conscious or no.

Dyson had no aspirations as a poet himself and never attempted, as did Parry with fairly dire results, to set his own texts to music. Where Dyson did excel, however, was in prose, in his use of English as an instrument of precision. In the sphere of music criticism there is, I dare say, no more supple, more lucid or less decorated prose than Dyson's at its best. His aim was always to express his meaning clearly, simply and exactly. In taking pleasure in writing he took pleasure in discipline, and would have been the first to agree with George Sampson that 'the nation that is muddled in its prose is muddled in its thoughts'. Dyson was celebrated for his unmuddled thinking and writing. Herbert Howells, opening the Regional Course in Music at St Paul's Girls' School on August 31 1951, said '... if you were luckier you'd look up and behold the lean, clear-cut features of Sir George Dyson. And in a few moments his keen mind would be shaping those incisive sentences that are characteristic of the man: sentences that seem to dot the lazy 'i's and cross the neglected 't's of one's own thoughts, ideas, theories and aspirations concerning the nature of one's work as a musician ...'.

Dyson knew that the best thing a pupil can get from a liberal education is not a mass of so-called authoritative information but the assurance that life is a great adventure worth pursuing in a spirit of discovery. But he was acutely conscious that enthusiasm cannot substitute for discipline; feeling must be embodied in form. There are few superfluous flowers of fancy in Dyson's writing on music. The mind is open and well-stocked, but the statements it formulates are always clear, concise and ordered, the prose plain and work-manlike: dry, perhaps, but like wine, not like bread or sawdust. In September 1932 Ernest Newman reviewed *The Progress of Music* in *The Sunday Times*. Having described Dyson as 'a fine scholar,

---

tenor solo, chorus and orchestra, Bunyan in *Men and Angels* (including 'Who would true valour see', also set by Dyson as No. 1 of the *Three Songs of Courage*), various Elizabethan poets in the *Six Pastorals* for solo vocal quartet, string quartet and piano. It is a pity that we never have a chance to hear these and other works by Walford Davies, for they look very attractive on the printed page.

a thinker, and a man of catholic tastes' he continues 'he writes in a curious staccato style that is the very thing for an author who wants to compress the maximum of information into the minimum of space. Every sentence is a short-distance shot that registers a hit: it reminds me of a workmanlike carpenter taking one bright new tack out of his mouth, placing it in the correct spot on the board without the slightest fumbling, and driving it home with one neat, decisive tap of the hammer. The style is just the thing for the matter.'

(iv)

Dyson was without exaggeration a brilliant man. He had exceptional mental alertness and strength and breadth of mind and was skilled in the general strategy and tactics of life in a way which few of his particular calling could rival. Many are the musicians who cannot in the wider sense be called educated. Delius complained bitterly of their endless 'shop-talk': remove which and they are uninteresting and uninterested. For Dyson, vocational studies and professional training were never a be-all and end-all. Here is part of a letter written to Freeman Dyson on March 6 1957 from Edinburgh, whither Dyson had travelled for a series of Carnegie Trust meetings:

> I have been writing my annual Trust speech, a nice mixed bag about (1) the equipment of small village halls. We have voted £100,000 to help them: heating, lighting, cooking apparatus, tables and chairs, etc. They are mainly halls we helped to build before the 1939 war, and in many cases their fittings and furniture are sadly deteriorated. We are already flooded with applications.
> (2) A scheme to encourage amateur scientific societies. Some of them are doing or want to do admirable local surveys: botany, geology, archaeology, and so forth, which are quite useful detailed supplements to the broader outlines of professional records. It is astonishing how many such groups there are, some of them of great repute, even in expert estimation. We want to help enthusiasts to attend courses at permanent Field Study centres, of which there are now five, with hostel accommodation and a professional panel of scientific instructors;
> and (3) a strong appeal for government help for art galleries and museums, some of the smaller of which have unique collections, but not even enough money to care for them. It is an acute problem in a country like England, which is so full of historical material.

22

At this moment in Winchester they are widening part of the High St. and our local museum Curator is overwhelmed with the search for and preservation of buried relics of 20 centuries. He has unearthed some most impressive specimens, XVIII century, mediaeval, Roman, down to prehistoric hearths and artifacts. He has a team of voluntary diggers, and it is quite a public entertainment to see them sifting every square inch of debris for coins, ornaments, glass, tiles, flints, bones, etc, some of them of outstanding interest. For the moment he can only label and store the stuff. How, when and where it can be properly sorted and displayed is a problem. And this is happening in many places elsewhere. We want the government to appoint a national body to control and subsidise the search and the preservation of what is found.

My speech will go to the press and may help to draw attention to the problem.

All this is a queer occupation for a musician, but I find it very absorbing and it brings me, and keeps me, in touch with a lot of very interesting people.

It is typical of Dyson that he was interested in others as much as, if not more than, himself. He never became a prisoner of his own career, never suffered that fatal loss of creative leisure, never lost heart, never became cynical or over-sophisticatedly worldly. I must quote wise Richard Church in his autobiographical *Voyage Home*:

... the only persons to escape a hardening of the arteries of the spirit are those who remain young, naïve, innocent, while maturing physically and mentally. They are 'the movers and shakers of the world forever, it seems'. They are the only people whose middle and late careers continue to reflect the sunrise, that under-lighting glory of wonder and novelty which alone makes life worth while, and also the story about it. Both success and failure are irrelevant issues, so long as the story continues to carry those early qualities of hope, of unfolding adventure, of discovery, and the perpetual struggle to understand what the whole experience signifies ...[11]

Dyson recognised that a man can have no greater happiness than to earn his living at a work which is also a vocation, and was duly thankful. His leisure, his happiness, were by-products of his individual personality, and the ordering of his life essentially a condition of mind dependent on humility. These are the matters which really count in the way a man's life evolves, and are of far deeper import than social conditions, accidents of family inheritance,

---

11. London 1964, pp. 104–5

23

the unpredictabilities of economic environment, and any number of other external and largely irrelevant considerations. The life of a man like Dyson, which appears to bear no relation to the circumstances and heredity into which he was born, surely proves this conclusively.

(v)

Said Sir Thomas Browne, the physician of 17th-century Norwich (of *Religio Medici* fame): 'the iniquity of oblivion blindly scattereth her poppy, and deals with the memory of men without distinction to merit of perpetuity.' Dyson composed a wealth of beautiful music, and his words are plenteous in wisdom and wit. Yet since his death in 1964 little has been heard of him, and even less of his music. No doubt his Englishness is one obstacle, his traditionalism another. Yet these are precisely the qualities which make him attractive to those with conservative inclinations and a strong sense of the past, and of home. I have never felt there to be anything provincial or self-conscious about Dyson's Englishness. At its best it simply represents the character and culture of England − if by that we understand, as I think Dyson did, a marriage of language, landscape, buildings and music with people and politics. Dyson was aware of fashion but chose instead to follow instinctive feeling, based on ancestral and inherited experience: in other words tradition. There is a lovely truth and clarity in all Dyson, words and music. Richard Church, lecturing at the University of Heidelberg on 'The Central English Flavour', described how here and there an individual creative craftsman in whatever artistic discipline

> ... stands aside like an ancient and tribal monolith, and is an object for amusement to the clever fashionables. But to people at home, the naïve and deep-rooted folk who are still creatures of the community where they and their ancestors have been rooted for generations, those individual craftsmen are not unwelcome. They are, as it were, milestones to reality. They make the quiet, stay-at-home folk appreciate, and appreciate with certainty, where they still belong in a world of confusion and international uproar ... quiet, sane, stable spokesmen of a way of life that is centuries deep within the confinement of your national tradition; a tradition like a garden where every plant, every flower is known to you, and cherished accordingly; not only for its present beauty, but for its reminder of an intimate past, of hands

24

that planted it, and made a landscape whose features are significant to *you*, and to *you* alone, as Germans, Swedes or Danes – or English or French: all folk within their own ancient cultural community, each a ripe civilization not lightly to be uprooted ...[12]

Dyson, like several of the English writers Church had specifically in mind – Edmund Blunden, Frank Kendon, H.E. Bates – was a man of the people. He knew the problems of early poverty, struggle, adversity; he had fought the fight of a marked sensibility against a crude and hostile environment. He was thereby enabled to strike at the heart of the matter, the crux of English life, the roots, the soil, the age and permanence of things. He never fell from grace, his perception of the world as a wonderful and beautiful place remained untarnished. In a sense he was an innocent. We can learn much about his essential nature if we compare him with his favourite poet, Herrick. We can easily see *why* he was his favourite. Some composers have desired grandly, some modestly. Their desires are contained in their music for all to hear. Dyson is not among the great composers, and his desires, as his music reflects them, are not imperial. Masefield wrote of Herrick that he

> seems to have desired a little house not far from London, with a little garden, which, in summer, would have been fragrant with many roses, red and white. The rooms of the house would have been sweet with perfumes, with musk, and crushed amber, and civet, and ambergris, and myrrh. In one of the rooms there would have been a few choice books: an Anacreon, a Catullus, and that Propertius to whom he once pledged a tun. This room would have needed a bronze Bacchus, and a flagon for sack, and a chair for a poetical friend. He would have been well content to sit in such a room for ever, with the canary within reach, and the incense wreathing round the bronze, had it been granted to him to hear the voice of Julia 'melting melodious words to Lutes of Amber' or to see her passing in the garden, when he looked up to think of a rhyme.

Mutatis mutandis this sounds like Dyson's Delight to a 'D' (or should it be 'G.D.'?) as those who have sat in his little house in Winchester, 'not far from London, with a little garden ...', will know. The 'few choice books' – mainly poetry, some history – are there, and the 'chair for a poetical friend'. There is little passion in Dyson, less in Herrick, rather a sustained exercise of the purely musical, poetical

---

12. Printed in *Speaking Aloud* (London 1968, p.14)

and intuitive faculties. Perhaps 'gusto' is a good word, the passion of the connoisseur. There is joy and gladness, the singing of one with no fear of old age: spring-blitheness, and autumnal ripeness rather than nostalgia:

Whán that Aprillé with hise showès soote
The droghte of March hath percèd to the roote
And bathéd every veyne in swich licóur
Of which vertú engendered is the flour ...

Dyson's music is the result of a particularly felicitous combination of natural inspiration and conscious craftsmanship; and we may perhaps draw a parallel between Herrick's early experience as apprentice to his uncle, a goldsmith in Cheapside, and Dyson's being raised by a blacksmith father and a weaver mother (the latter puts in a brief appearance in Portrait VII of *The Canterbury Pilgrims* as part of the Haberdasher and his Fraternity). Pride in fine workmanship is everywhere apparent, in Dyson as in Herrick, likewise grace of expression and candour of spirit, and the rare gift of combining youthful beauty with age-old wisdom. They both have unfailing freshness, easy fitness in language, unforced and delightful melody. They share a tendency to blandness, to a certain 'mellisonant' monotony; and it is as true of Dyson, as of Herrick, that his best-known work (*The Canterbury Pilgrims*) is not in all particulars his best.

There is, too, the question of religion. Some find it surprising that Vaughan Williams, a man who cared passionately all his life about hymns and carols, and spent so much of his time setting to music Herbert and Bunyan, the Bible and the Liturgy, was a youthful atheist and lifelong agnostic. Dyson, who also set hymns, carols, Herbert and Bunyan, the Bible and the Liturgy, was similarly never a 'religious' man in the conventional sense. Nor were Parry, Howells, Finzi or Bax. Yet from this galaxy of 'unbelievers' has issued some of the most inspiring 'religious' music of the century − *The Pilgrim's Progress* (Vaughan Williams), Dyson's own *Quo Vadis* and *Hierusalem, Songs of Farewell* (Parry), *Hymnus Paradisi* (Howells), *Dies Natalis* (Finzi), *Mater Ora Filium* (Bax). Dyson's 'church' music is a vehicle for ideas and feelings rather than for beliefs. He had as we know a profound feeling for tradition: for English language and

26

literature; (the Bible and the Book of Common Prayer contain, after all, some of the finest prose in the language); he had no less profound a sense of quality, and of spiritual values. He never made public property of his religion, but hymns of one sort or another played a large part in his composing. Setting hymns means writing tunes for massed singing, one of the most difficult feats for any composer to perform. Dyson had hs share of failures, but some notable successes, eg:

Now the words of these and suchlike hymns are among those which, passing on from generation to generation, have helped to form the texture of the English mind. George Sampson, in his essay 'The Century of Divine Songs',[13] speaks of the way a congregational hymn can create the sense of belonging to a continuing fellowship: 'A hymn is a mystical poem, full of symbols which give us a hold upon that continuity, or immensity, or eternity, from which we cannot be cut off without being lost in a world of other lost creatures ... The sense of restoration to our own true home and family animates the six-and-twenty stanzas of that wonderful 16th-century hymn:

Hierusalem, my happy home,
When shall I come to thee?
When shall my labours have an end?
Thy Joys when shall I see?'

13. Printed in *Seven Essays* (Cambridge 1947, pp. 229–231)

Dyson's glowing setting of this hymn — his last major work — was made in retirement at Winchester. Here it was that *he* felt, evidently, the 'sense of restoration to his own home and family'; hence the last late but luxuriant flowering of his talent.

In this connection Herrick is relevant. For a long time Herrick's religious poetry was derided. Now it is seen more as part of a 17th-century Anglican attempt to idealise childhood in the face of the Puritan view, which was of the child lost in original sin and a prey to deadly corruption. Dyson's Christian is, one feels, more akin to Bunyan's. 'The name of the chamber was peace, where he slept all night till break of day, and then he awoke and sang.'[14]

Both Herrick and Dyson suffered in their own time from being derided as old-fashioned. But what matters is that Dyson wrote the music he wanted to write, which was not necessarily that which contemporary critics wanted him to write; and that he communicated musical matter of sufficient validity to rouse many musical people, both amateur and professional, to a high degree of enthusiasm, however unmodish the style he employed to do so. I have often wondered if Dyson knew of the marvellous novel by Rose Macaulay written in 1932 and called *They were Defeated*. It is her only historical novel and was born of her sympathy for the seventeenth century and for the stoics and poets and scholars whose harmless lives were disrupted by the Civil War. One of them was Robert Herrick (a distant relation of Rose Macaulay), who presides over the book. The scene moves between Devonshire and Cambridge: Herrick revisits his old University,[15] where he is politely made to feel of small account:

---

14. George Sampson in his *English for the English* (Cambridge 1921) quotes some lines from the 'Benedictus':

> Through the tender mercy of our God, whereby the day-spring from on high hath visited us,
>
> To give light to them that sit in darkness and in the shadow of death, and to guide our feet into the way of peace.

'Do we', he asks, 'ever stay to dwell on the loveliness of a passage like that, in which almost every word is a poem, or do we not just go passively through it as a hustled tourist goes through a picture-gallery, encompassed with beauty and seeing almost nothing?' If Dyson's setting of these words in his Morning Service in F cannot make us 'dwell on its loveliness', nothing can.

15. Where for a time he attended my own college, Trinity Hall. More than 300 years

contemporary intellectual tendencies favour the Metaphysicals, the younger poets are condescending. At the end

> Mr Herrick saw Cambridge as gone utterly into chaos, darkness and ignominy, like the Church, like the country, like the times. Yet he would still be a poet, still wear, whether mortals conceded it him or not, his little parsley crown. Still the pastoral country smiled, and flowers blew; still, though may-poles were down and midsummer bonfires extinguished, the may flowered white on the back, and girls and boys would go a-maying, and the June country smell of hay, and the elves dance beneath the moon ...

Dyson, like Herrick, represents something permanent in the spirit of music, of poetry and of England:

> Thou shalt not all die; for while Love's fire shines
> Upon his altar, men shall read thy lines;
> And learn'd musicians shall, to honour Herrick's
> Fame, and his name, both set and sing his lyrics.

*   *   *   *   *

In compiling this anthology of Dyson's writings, lectures and broadcasts I have limited my editorial activity for the most part to selecting and cutting. However, those of the broadcast scripts which were delivered extempore at the microphone needed a small amount of cosmetic retouching here and there, and made better sense for the occasional music-type example replacing live illustration.[16] Looking at the collection as a whole we can only regret that Dyson did not write in more detail on certain composers he particularly admired (e.g., Delius and Vaughan Williams) and that he never, as far as I know, went into print at all on the subject

---

later I was mindful of this in the summer of 1986 when, en route for nearby St Catharine's to make a recording of Dyson's church and organ music, I made a special detour in order to pass through the grounds of Trinity Hall.

16. Dyson's outstanding gifts as a broadcaster were early recognised. In the late 1920s concern was caused in the BBC Music Department by the reported (though no doubt publicly unprintable) opinion of Delius on musical appreciation talks. It was felt that Dyson should be asked to give the ordinary listener help and guidance on modern music. 'I think there is a general consensus about Dr Dyson — he is regarded as the best man both by Sir Hugh Allen and Ernest Newman, who usually don't agree on anything. He is a first-rate broadcaster ...' (Internal Circulating Memo dated 24 October 1929)

of Parry, by whom he was greatly influenced both musically and generally. However, on general musical topics he offers a wealth of material for our entertainment and edification. If there is one part of this anthology to which I suspect readers will return more frequently than to any other, it is the unlikeliest: the College Addresses. Merely to dip into these is at once to perceive their sterling superiority to most others of their ilk. Here is no pompous preaching, platidunizing or patronising, but instead a sympathetic and attractive combination of idealism and common sense. The interest and application of these talks is restricted neither to musicians, nor to those of student age; and to a modern generation unused to war they unwittingly convey a strong sense of atmosphere: this, apparently, was really what it was like trying to keep ordinary life and work afloat at a time of great danger and upheaval. Uncertainty and tragedy were everyone's imminent daily lot, but the spirit was willing enough to survive.

In Dyson we had a man of learning, humanity and charm, who for nearly 50 years spent time and energy he might well have devoted to composition making musical England a fit place to live in. Let us show our gratitude first and foremost by bringing his music back into the repertoire. Thanks to him and others like him we could slightly paraphrase *The Tempest* and say:

> This isle is fuller of noises,
> Sounds and sweet airs, that give delight,
>   and hurt not.

CHRISTOPHER PALMER
London, Maida Vale
May 1988

30

Autobiographical

My boyhood was spent in a busy industrial town of the West Riding in the days of the butterfly gas-burner and the horse omnibus. We made our music on the cottage piano, the church or chapel organ, and by the voices of many choirs. There was a good choral society in our town and a struggling amateur orchestra. We had in our neighbourhood what we held to be the finest brass band in the world, Black Dyke, and a number of others of second rank. The only professional orchestra of standing, the Hallé, was thirty miles away at Manchester. I devoured all the piano music I could get hold of, I learnt the classical overtures and symphonies as piano duets, and I played through all the Beethoven violin sonatas with a young friend, more than once, at a sitting. I doubt if there is today any adequate substitute for this digging out of music with one's own hands. Our field may have been narrow, but it was exact and intense. Our choral tradition was Handel, Mendelssohn, and the usual anthems and part-songs. I first heard Wagner on a brass band. Only very occasionally did the Hallé orchestra come within reach, and the experience was bewildering in its wealth of colour and complication of sound. I remember being completely dazed by the 'Meistersinger' overture under Richter.

I played services on the organ from the age of thirteen, and at sixteen I became a Fellow of the Royal College of Organists and an open scholar at the Royal College of Music. This latter award brought me to London in 1900, and I spent four years at the Royal College, my most powerful and exacting teacher being Sir Charles Stanford. I played the organ at Greenwich Parish Church and made a few extra pounds by playing drums and 'effects' occasionally at a theatre or concert. Edgar Bainton, Frank Bridge, Rutland Boughton, Thomas Dunhill, and John Ireland were among my composer contemporaries, and I learnt a great deal from them. There were no local or state grants for maintenance in those days and most of us had to count our pence. I was a very fluent reader and in the London of that time, as at home, we learnt most of our music by playing it ourselves in any combination

31

we could muster. Our highlights were orchestral concerts, the gallery at Covent Garden, and the occasional orgy of London rehearsals for a provincial festival. I wrote student compositions which were considered promising, and I still vividly remember some of the music written by my fellow-students. What I owe to the Royal College and to my teachers and contemporaries will fill most of this book.

In 1904 I was elected to the Mendelssohn scholarship. This sent me abroad, and my intention was to go and study in Leipzig. Stanford dissuaded me. He said I had had enough teaching. 'Go to Italy, my boy, and sit in the sun.' I did, and I have since given the same refreshing advice to other young musicians, with happy results. There was Buonamici in Florence, Sgambati in Rome and Martucci in Naples. I spent most of my time in Florence and Rome. Sgambati was kind to me, as were many English and Italian musical residents everywhere. It was Martucci who conducted the first performance in Italy of Richard Strauss's *Don Juan*. The audience booed and hissed until he stopped the performance and shouted: 'E scritto cosii!' (It's written so). I saw the first performance of Giordano's *Siberia*, of which the second act is a most moving procession of Russian prisoners in the snow. The audience insisted on a complete repetition of the whole act! Later I heard the first performance in Italy of the St. Matthew Passion by a choir from Zürich in Milan. The Italian audience was true to type. Every telling phrase received half-suppressed 'bravos', and the 'thunder and lightning' chorus had to be repeated. They were good people to live with, friendly and uninhibited.

But my most memorable good fortune in Italy was the interest and kindness of the family of the Countess Clara Gigliucci, a wonderful old lady who, as Clara Novello, had been one of the most famous singers in Europe half a century before. She was nearly ninety. Her father was Vincent Novello, the founder of the famous firm of music publishers, and to the house where she lived as a child in London came Keats and Shelley, Leigh Hunt and Charles Lamb. Lamb wrote a little poem about her singing, containing the lines:

Women lead men by the nose, some cynics say;
You draw them by the ears – a delicater way.

She was a contemporary of Mendelssohn, Chopin, Schumann, Wagner, and Liszt. She had danced in Paris to Chopin's playing.

She had sung Rossini's operas when he was at the height of his fame. She sang the soprano solos in the first performance in England of Beethoven's Mass in D in 1832. She had been a prima donna in the chief festivals and opera-houses of Europe. She had known old gentlemen who had sung in the first Handel festival of 1784.

To be with her was like travelling back a whole century. Mendelssohn was her most vivid memory, and she spoke of him, Felix, as if he had only lately left the world, and left it unutterably poorer. I played to her, even venturing as far as Debussy. It was most moving to feel that in her presence one could bring Debussy almost within speaking distance of Handel. One omission I have never ceased to regret. I was then too young to realize it, but if only I had taken to her a copy of *The Messiah* one evening, and asked how and to what extent the singers nearest to Handel had modified or embellished his recitatives, I should have been able to resolve many of the doubts which have harassed a century of editors and singers.

I spent some time in Vienna, and many months in Berlin and Dresden. In Berlin I was in time to meet Joachim and listen to the private rehearsals of his quartet. I visited the home of Richard Strauss, then at the height of his creative and directive powers. Mottl, Steinberg, Weingartner, and Nikisch, with Strauss himself, were the leading conductors. I saw *Salome* in its early days in Dresden, and heard the story of a dress rehearsal when Frau von Wittich, in the title-part, could not hold some of the more dissonant notes. Von Schuch, the conductor, got more and more irritated and exacting, until Strauss himself intervened and said: 'It doesn't matter at all, and it sounds lovely.' Forty years later, in London, he talked to me of those exciting days when *Salome* and *Elektra* were new.[1]

I wrote a number of compositions during this period, one of which, a rather blatant symphonic poem called *Siena*, I was recalled to London to conduct. Ernest Newman said it ought to be 'burnt', but Nikisch put it in one of his programmes and directed it most sympathetically.[2] All these manuscripts have long gone. I returned

---

1. This was in October 1947, when at the age of 83 he came to London (for the first time since before the war) to take part in a special Strauss festival planned by Sir Thomas Beecham.
2. Dyson's programme-note for his own first performance of this three-movement

permanently to England late in 1907 and, having been long absent, and composition being in those days the most precarious of all ventures, it was some time before I found work on which I could live. It was Sir Hubert Parry, the Director of the Royal College of Music, who sent me to the Royal Naval College at Osborne, and thus began nearly thirty years' work in schools. Their Lordships of the Admiralty had concurred that young naval cadets might well be given a chance to develop any musical leanings they might have, for their lives would be spent under conditions in which they would have to rely largely on themselves for recreation and entertainment. I was

---

work (Queen's Hall, 11 July 1907, with the LSO) has survived, even though the work itself has not! It is interesting enough to be worth reproducing:

'The work is an attempt to portray the atmosphere of the race for the 'Palio', or standard, which takes place annually in Siena on the Feast of the Assumption. This race is one of the few remaining relics of pure mediaevalism, and although it has now lost its former religious significance, is still the great event of the year to the Sienese.

Eact Contrada, or division of the city, selects a horse, and the rivalry is so keen as to lead sometimes to serious disturbances. Each horse is led up to the altar of its patron church to be blessed, is then decked out in the gayest of trappings, and, followed by the representatives of the Contrada to which it belongs, is taken to the racecourse, if such a term may be so ill-applied. For the race is run round the Piazza in front of the municipal palace, and as this Piazza is in the shape of a half-moon, far from horizontal, and paved with cobbles, no more seemingly unfit place could well be imagined. Moreover, each jockey is allowed to carry a loaded stick, the starting apparatus is of the crudest description, and once the start has been made, no means, fair or foul, are considered disqualifying. The jockeys belabour one another unmercifully when chance occurs, and but for their steel caps and shoulder-plates, would often be seriously injured. Altogether, the function is a mad riot, rather than a race, and, run under the fierce summer sun of Italy, would be humorous, were it not for the occasionally tragic consequences.

The music merely follows the events of the day, the short introduction being founded on themes taken from the march played on the occasion.

I. The race is preceded by a procession, in which the flamboyant costumes and gorgeous standards of each Contrada, together with the coveted 'Palio' itself, are displayed.

II. The course is cleared, and a trumpet call announces the beginning of the race. Three times round the Piazza is the length of the course, and a second fanfare proclaims the winner.

III. An Intermezzo follows, and the day ends with a riotous banquet. The winning jockey is the hero of the feast, and his horse is placed at the head of the table, where he enjoys to the full the endless sweetmeats which are his portion.'

34

a decided innovation, but the four hundred boys were very bright specimens, with the usual sprinkling of musical talent and scores of good voices. Two young princes, afterwards King Edward VIII and King George VI, were among them. There was a large naval and civilian staff, and we soon had a good choir and some quite accomplished soloists. We sang cantatas and had periodical stage shows, writing our own words and music, with a workshop of naval engineers to design and rig the settings. There were boats and launches on the Solent to play with, and the Commander-in-Chief at Portsmouth had the genial habit of occasionally lending us a torpedo-boat, complete with crew, food, and astonishing speed, for a day's 'choir-outing'. Those were very happy years for us all.

We had no prevision of the war that was to come, in which some of our officers were to reach high rank, and some, with a sadly large number of our cadets, were to be lost. Only when the war came did we realize that Osborne itself, which doubled the entry of cadets into the Navy, was founded by the Admiralty in foresight of the struggle that might lie ahead. After the war the Osborne College was closed, and the buildings dismantled.

In 1911 I went to Marlborough College and from 1914 to 1920 I was in and out of the war. I began in the infantry and by a sheer accident of official choice I was pushed into training men to use hand grenades. There was no manual on the subject, and I therefore set down in writing and diagram some of the exercises we extemporized. These were published and circulated both in our own army and in America and gave me a martial reputation which was quite incongruous and still occasionally dogs me. I came back from France in 1916 and was for a long time convalescent. Again chance intervened and I began, as a form of mild occupation, to dabble in financial law in a lawyer friend's office. I was found to have a flair for figures and I helped to prepare cases for the Board of Referees under the Finance Act of 1915. I had for a time serious thoughts of forsaking music permanently and reading for the Bar. But my next task was two years in the Air Ministry, while the accumulated material of the war was being destroyed or dispersed. This occupied me until the end of 1920 and had two or three musical incidents. I prepared the establishment of the

R.A.F. military bands, I edited a set of bugle-calls, and I issued and in part composed the R.A.F. March Past. Sir Walford Davies had written a piano sketch of a short quick march. I added the broader tune in the middle, scored it, and had it played to the appropriate officers in the Ministry. They approved and adopted it as it now stands.

These six queer years of upheaval came to an end when I was invited to take charge of the music at Wellington College at the beginning of 1921. At odd intervals during the war period I had made a fairly exhaustive study of the more extreme revolutions in contemporary music. In 1921 I began to lecture on the subject, and my memory was equal to playing substantial illustrations from many sources. I was encouraged to write a book, which became *The New Music*, published in 1923. I am told it is still up-to-date in its general and technical classifications, for nothing has happened since that was not implicit in the music written before 1920.

In 1924 I moved to Winchester College, and it was there that all my varied musical activities and experiences coalesced into a most happy and busy life. I had a choir of choristers and lay clerks, supplemented by a picked few from the school. We could sing music from the Tudor period to our own day. I had a school orchestra and a school chorus. I had a city orchestra, including most of the good string players from twenty miles around, and we brought down London Symphony wind for our concerts. I had also an adult choral society, carefully selected and balanced. And we all supported our annual Winchester Festival. I found time to give University lectures occasionally, and I took over from Sir Walford Davies his inimitable series of broadcasts: 'Music and the ordinary listener'. I gave this weekly broadcast for two years, combining it with a pleasant day's teaching at the Royal College. It seems, in retrospect, as though no normal time-table could be made to include all this, but I think the long frustration of the war had made us all exceptionally keen and resilient. I have since found my students, coming back from military service, similarly enthusiastic and indefatigable.

And this is not all, for I wrote a second book: *The Progress of Music*, dealing with the historical and social background of music which I had described in some of my broadcasts, and I began again seriously to compose. *In Honour of the City*, a choral setting of Dunbar's poem, came first, and then I spent the scattered hours of two years on my setting of the Prologue to Chaucer's *Canterbury Tales*. The *Canterbury Pilgrims* have gone round the English-speaking world, and this work is the basis of such repute as I possess. It was written for my friends of the Winchester Festival. I wrote one work for Leeds and several for the Three Choirs, the oldest and to me the most congenial musical gathering in England. I wrote a symphony, a violin concerto, and many smaller pieces of all kinds including a large group of songs for massed singing.[3]

My repute is that of a good technician, happy with words, but not markedly original. I am familiar with modern idioms, but they are outside the vocabulary of what I want to say. I am really what the eighteenth century called a *Kapellmeister*, an untranslatable word which means a musician equipped both to compose and produce such music as is needed in his position or environment. He and his patrons looked on musical composition, not as a remote and exceptional activity, but as a matter of everyday use and wont. They asked for

---

3. Dyson spent the intervals of three busy years (1929–31) preparing *The Canterbury Pilgrims* – a year of sketches, a year writing the full choral-orchestral score of nearly 400 pages, and the best part of a year overseeing the production of the material. Thirty years later, in 1960, he wrote to Freeman 'That work lives as nothing else I have done ... it really is becoming a standard among the choral societies, a prophecy made by Sir Henry Wood 25 years ago ... the audiences seem to like it, and so do the performers, and it is a major satisfaction to me in these quiet years.' In November 1963 (he was now 80) he wrote to his publisher 'I have been looking into my records, and I find that the two editions of *The Canterbury Pilgrims*, combined, have passed the 20,000 mark, and *In Honour of the City* has sold over 15,000. *At the Tabard Inn* seems to be doing pretty well too, in performances. All of which naturally pleases me, and I hope you too.' The work for Leeds was *The Blacksmiths* (1934); *St Paul's Voyage to Melita* was written for the 1933 Three Choirs Festival at Hereford, *Nebuchadnezzar* for Worcester in 1935. *Quo Vadis* (in two parts) spanned the war years and was first performed complete at Hereford in 1948. (See illustration on p. 000). The Violin Concerto of 1942 was composed in memory of W. H. ('Billy') Reed, Dyson's affectionate memoir of whom is printed on p. 169. Of the 'smaller pieces of all kinds' the twin Concerti for Strings – the *Concerto da Camera* and *Concerto da Chiesa* – should be mentioned, likewise the *Concerto Leggiero* for piano and strings. There is a small but select quantity of church music, and a number of attractive choral suites for differing vocal combinations.

new music for every occasion. Speed and good craftsmanship were their primary needs. The *Kapellmeister* type still exists, but his function has now been largely filled by the music library, the whole body of music from the past which we preserve and use for all purposes. Fluent craftsmanship is still demanded for light music, background music, and films. But serious 'concert' music has to be different, more exceptional, more personal and individual in style.

For fifteen years I was Director of the Royal College of Music, the first child of the place to reach that office. I was born in the year of its foundation. During these years I have been very near the centre of that enormous web of endeavour which is music in Britain. I have helped to organize and administer every kind of musical enterprise, and I have been close to all the larger problems of policy and patronage which affect the art and the profession. I have been able to observe at first hand the methods and effects of our educational system, both general and specialist, on the world of music as a whole, and I have known every type of artist, teacher, and student.

All writing is to some extent autobiography, for the writer selects both his facts and his fancies, and these will reflect his personality and opinions. I have set down the broad outline of my own education and experience because this inevitably determines the range and validity of any views I may express. I am conscious of certain very definite predispositions. The worst performances of opera I have ever heard took place in the more obscure theatres of Italy, the dullest concerts in the smaller towns of Germany. But from these sources were recruited the composers and performers who became the giants of the profession. I cannot look upon music as a metropolitan art, consisting solely of the select and highly specialized. Music is of the people, and genius is as likely to be born in a country village as in a capital city. Indeed most of the greater artists of the world came from small places. That is why we should never forget the amateur, and particularly the provincial amateur. It is he who provides the broad foundation of national discrimination and taste. It is in his home or among his circle that many talents are first found. Add to this the social value of any corporate artistic activity and we reach what I feel to be the ultimate purpose of all the arts. They are not merely the gifts and privileges of the few. They are a potential way of life for everyone, a part of our social sanity and the foundation of our active and recuperative leisure.

(from *Fiddling while Rome Burns*)

College Addresses, 1938 – 1949
(a selection)

My first concern to-day is to pay the tribute of a few words to the memory of a life-long servant of this College, Bernard Parker, our caretaker, who died peacefully after a short illness, on 27th December. He died as he would have wished, still caring for everything we value in this place, and still sheltered by these walls, which made his home.

To most of you he appeared a frail and ageing figure, cheerfully smiling and nodding the answers to questions he found it increasingly difficult to hear. When I first came to this College, 37 years ago, none of the teaching rooms were heated, and Parker's task was to keep these 50 or 60 open coal fires burning. Hour after hour, and day after day, he trudged patiently and cheerfully up our five long flights of stairs, carrying coals, in order that we might teach and be taught in tolerable comfort.

Before that he had blown the old hand-blown organs on which a whole generation of organists learnt their work. You may have seen in *The Times* the statement that Parker was one of the most accurate and exacting judges of organ-playing that we have ever had. That statement is perfectly true, and to the end of his days he never forgot a note of that great body of classical organ-music which he had thus learnt in his youth.

For 54 years he served this place, and I know you would like me to record our regard and gratitude for his life and work, and our deep sympathy with Mrs Parker, also for many years our friend and helper in this place, whose loss cannot be expressed in words.

And I should like to add a few more general thoughts which arise from this loss we have sustained. We who devote ourselves to the arts should never forget that we cannot exist at all unless our material needs are provided for by the labour of others. The arts only begin when society has organised itself in such a way that we can have freedom and leisure to pursue our vocations, while other members of the community provide for our material needs. This freedom of ours is bought for us by their labour, or by the labour of the machines which they tend. We owe them a never-failing respect and consideration.

Nor is this the whole story. In an institution like this College, there has to be an administrative staff who arrange the details of our studies, our times and places and meetings, the care of our instruments and books, the thousand and one items of organisation, financial, clerical and material, without which none of us could either teach or be taught efficiently. I should like it to be a feature of this College that nobody ever fails in consideration and appreciation of all these services; that we none of us ever give unnecessary trouble to those who work for us; that we never leave them to do anything that we can do ourselves; that we all co-operate to the best of our power in making our domestic and administrative machinery work as smoothly and easily as is humanly possible. I am sure I can count on you in this, and the easier it is to organise ourselves, the more and the better will be our music.

I come now to the thought that is uppermost in all our minds. Sir Hugh Allen has left us. He has chosen to retire from the Directorship while he is still of an age and vigour that secures for many years to come his position as chief 'elder statesman' of our national music. We all miss him and shall continue to miss him, nobody more than I. But it would be a poor tribute to his reign if we were to think that his dynamic personality, his creative energy, and his broad humanity, would not continue for a very long time to mould and influence the prevailing spirit of this place. We are all going to work as if the volcanic drive of Sir Hugh were still at our backs. Every spot and every department in this College bears the imprint of his unique mind and heart. We are going to keep and treasure this heritage, to consolidate these his aims and ideals. That is the response he would desire. That is the least we can give him.

Too often the Founders of an institution are dim historical figures whom we find it very difficult to clothe with reality. Sir Hugh is in strict truth one of our Founders. He did not create the College, but he has done more than any other one man to make it the institution it now is. Let us tell him so, and let us assure him of our gratitude, our respect and our affection, and wish him the long life, health and happiness that he has so finely earned.

Lastly, a word about me, not so much about me personally, as about the change of which I am the portent. I suppose I am what the Americans would call the 'New Deal.' And I am new in two senses. I am not only a new Director, but a new kind of Director. Many years ago I went to work in a new School, and we used to say then, 'The test of this place will come when these boys grow up and come back as masters, possibly headmasters.' That is the stage this Royal College has now reached. I come back as an Old Boy, the first Old Boy who has been chosen to be Director, and I take my appointment to be not so much a tribute to me, though I am naturally proud of it, but as a tribute to the whole generation of students which I represent. The College has grown its own staff, its own Head. That process will continue, we hope, and I am probably talking this morning to some who will in time join our staff of Professors, and possibly to one or more who may ultimately take my place.

Now we all know something of the 'Old School Tie.' We have most of us met those choleric 'Old Boys' who come down and say: 'What was good enough for me ought to be good enough for you.' And I want in this, my first address to you, to make it clear at once that in my opinion what was good enough for students in this place 30 years ago is nothing like good enough for you now. I will try to tell you why in a moment.

For myself I have come back to learn. This College is full of activities that did not exist at all in my student days. I have come to learn, and I am going to enjoy learning. I think this is the ninth or tenth time, in a somewhat wandering career, that I have had to face and try to comprehend a new sphere of work. One learns, I hope, a certain amount of wisdom by these removals. One learns to winnow one's belongings, get rid of obsolete books, abandon or replace decrepit furniture, and so forth. And one learns too, I trust, to winnow one's mind, to get rid of preconceived ideas, obsolete methods, particular shibboleths and prejudices. No two institutions in the world are alike. My first task is to get to know this College, not as it was thirty years ago, but as it is now. Only then shall I be competent to apply any ideas I may have as to its future.

I said just now that what was good enough for us is not good enough for you. I will give you two reasons, among many. You may find it hard to believe, but I was once knocked over in the street by

41

a cart-horse (No, I was quite teetotal then). I have heard young friends ask: 'How on earth did people ever manage to get run over by a four wheeled horse-cart?' Well, they did. Traffic ran then at a mere five or six miles an hour, and yet we loitered or ambled about in the streets so carelessly that we occasionally got run over. In the streets to-day, as you know, there are only two kinds of people, the quick and the dead. And that is true not only of the highways of traffic, it is true also of the highways of commerce, of politics, of science, even of the arts and crafts. Your artistic equipment has got to be made so efficient, so resilient, so keyed-up, that you can go forth into this incomparably swifter world of to-day and neither be left behind nor run over.

My second reason for desiring that you should have the best possible preparation we can give you is this. When I left this College in 1904, I went out into a comparatively silent world. My first appointment was in a small place, and in that place I made music, and made music that had not existed there before. I was my own standard, and it was then comparatively easy for the musician of professional training to make a considerable reputation in the smaller towns and institutions. You have no such easy task. If you go and play the piano, even in a remote village, people will not compare you with, say, the rector's daughter or the young man in the music shop. They will say: 'Oh, yes, she plays quite well, but I'd rather hear Myra Hess on the wireless.' You will be thus pitted against the greatest artists in the world, who broadcast or make gramophone records. And that is a very serious competition indeed, and one which is likely to become more severe rather than less.

I am not suggesting that any wireless or mechanical performance is as good as an equal performance in the flesh. But the machines are getting steadily better, and their best is certainly far better, to the normal listener, than a second-rate performance at first hand, however earnest and well-meaning. What then is the reply to these ubiquitous and ever-improving machines? There is to my mind one answer only. You can never beat a machine on its own ground. You must choose a ground where the machine fails. And the machine as we have it fails in the combined personal and musical contact which only a living and present artist can give. You have to be more and ever more musical, and you have to convey in some mysterious

42

fashion, by your direct and personal art, that feeling of sympathetic understanding and community of aesthetic feeling which will bring your music convincingly and irresistibly before those, be they few or many, amongst whom your work is cast.

And here I come back to Sir Hugh's broad humanity. Why should people care about your special talent, which is music, if you care not at all about their special talents or preoccupations? Wherever you go you will be a member of a community. You will get from that community what you give to it, neither more nor less. And the first gift is sympathy, understanding, humanity. We are not, I hope, isolated and queer people living a parasitic life in an artificial society. We are 'citizens of no mean city,' members of a world-wide community, practitioners in the most universal of all the arts. Our knowledge, our understanding, and our devotion must be equally wide, equally generous and equally human.

September 1938

During the last few days I have felt that I might perhaps say something in this address about our present national anxieties. It will be twenty years this term since the War of 1914–1918 came to an end. Those of us who lived through that period are permanently marked by it. And whatever may be your views of the issues that confront us to-day I would ask you to remember that there is no responsible statesman in Europe who has not experienced at first hand the slaughter and devastation of war. It is impossible to believe that these men, whatever their political complexion, would lightly give rein to that insane waste and fury which war inevitably brings.

There are just two things I should like to say on this subject. The first is that neither war nor peace are simple issues. They are both, in essence, states of the mind and heart. A man can be a soldier by profession and yet have neither bitterness nor hatred in his heart. There are names inscribed in our entrance hall, young men who fought twenty years ago, not because they hated their enemies, but because they could not desert their friends. I talked to one of them only a very short time before he was killed. He was an artist, a peace-lover, a mind quite untarnished, who yet kept his soldier's course. He could not stand aside and let others face

43

danger in his stead. There were a great many such men of peace in the trenches in France.

And peace too is a state of the soul. There are men who profess peace and yet seem totally incapable of it, who cannot admit an honest difference of opinion, who cannot see any worthy motive outside their own class or clan. What one man calls peace may be to another stagnation, or indifference, or even permanent injustice. None of these problems are simple, and the most we can any of us do is to keep our minds broad in understanding, our hearts open and unembittered. Few of us can know all the facts. Few of us could bear the responsibility of events. Let us at least give room for genuine and deep concern to those who have to think and act for us, on the nation's behalf.

Our own immediate duties are clear enough. In so far and for so long as our civilisation allows us to devote ourselves to our art, that is our sphere. Let us make the most of it. If other tasks should come to us, then we shall do them too, I trust, as well as we can. I am not a pessimist, even in foreign affairs. Twenty-four years ago it seemed as though everything we loved best had come to an end. You in this Hall to-day, with your youth, your talents and your enthusiasm, prove how wrong we were. The future is always uncertain. But though it may sometimes come short of our hopes, it is usually far better than our fears. Your business is to fit yourselves for a high profession, a profession which demands ever more and more concentration and talent. This College is here to help you, and we ask you to make the most you can of your opportunities ...

May 1939

During these holidays I recalled a holiday in 1913, now over twenty-five years ago, when I and two schoolmaster friends went to a London booking-office, asked for three single tickets to Moscow, were given them without any further formality, and set off to see what eastern Europe looked like. In those days you could go almost anywhere in the world without fuss or question. Russia was one of the few places where a passport was necessary, but it was a simple document, easy to get, and was hardly more than an identification paper in case you should need one for any official purpose.

We went through Holland, Germany, Poland, and back through Finland, Sweden and Norway. In southern Europe travel was equally informal; Spain, Italy, the Balkans. You hardly needed even to change your money. Sovereigns and five-pound notes, if you could muster any, were accepted without question anywhere. There was even a currency agreement by which Swiss, French or Italian francs were accepted mutually in all three countries. Almost the only limitation was that the Italians did not accept French coppers, or *vice versa*. It is a sad reflection on our so-called civilisation that these friendly relations have so tragically deteriorated.[1]

All the thoughtful people in the world are asking 'Why?' I wish I knew the answer. By some process of social and political change, by some spreading plague of jealousy and mistrust, the nations of Europe have built and are building ever higher walls round their separate domains, walls of ideas, of propaganda, of emotion, of tariffs and restrictions of all kinds, until it is almost impossible to believe that they were, only a comparatively short time ago, such tolerable and tolerant neighbours. And we cannot resist the conclusion that what has changed is the actual spirit of European intercourse, so far as this intercourse finds public expression.

Individually and personally considered, human nature is just what it was before. We meet people who, according to the present

---

1. Sixteen years later Dyson has occasion once more to recall these memories of his trip to Russia. On 26 March 1955 he wrote to Freeman in the U.S.A.:

'I felt it was not for me to interfere, or I should have written to you before this about the proposed visit to Russia. But now that you have settled the question yourself I want to tell you how profoundly relieved I am that you are not going. It simply is not worth the risk. Time after time they have turned what should have been a purely friendly exchange of information or collaboration into a political advertisement ... Oddly enough, the Russian problem has been in my mind in these last weeks because I have agreed to sponsor, with a short introductory speech, a series of Recitals on the B.B.C. Overseas Service, which goes behind the curtain and to the far east in general. One of the programmes is a Recital given by the best Russian violinist, David Oistrakh, who played in London last year. I told the Director of the B.B.C. service about my trip to Moscow 40 years ago, and how easy and friendly it was, and he said: Please say some of this when you introduce this Russian programme. So I did with a general plea for better manners and human faith across the political frontiers. It won't do any good, of course, as things are at present, but it may perhaps meet a few sympathetic ears on the other side ...'

temper of international politics, are held to be our bitter rivals, our implacable foes. Actually we find them pleasant, human, ordinary people, with their own particular likes and dislikes, but in no sense fundamentally different from the varied types we can find in our own parish. Talk to them of the normal ethical, intellectual or artistic values, and you find sympathy and agreement. They think of their friends and families as we think of ours. They love their literature, their art, their music, their science, just as we do. They may have gaps and stops in their minds which perplex us. But apparently we have traits which are just as inexplicable to them. But we do not therefore deliberately embitter one another. We do not whip out revolvers because Herr Solche and Monsieur Un Tel disagree about free trade. Signor Nessuno does not shoot me because I am lukewarm about his particular aspirations. In all our normal and personal relations with our fellow human-beings, of any language or of any colour, we may like or dislike, approve or disapprove, but we keep our tempers, we live and let live. And yet in the mass, in association, in parties, in regimented crowds, we seem to take on a new, an unyielding, an insistent and violent self-assertion, which becomes, in the domain of international politics, a fever of strife and enmity.

I believe this to be a main disease of our time. It is a psychological disease, an uncontrolled duality of character, which makes us at one moment good private neighbours, and at another, fierce public enemies. It has for long been a feature of our English public life, and one which has always amazed and perplexed foreigners, that two members of Parliament may call one another the most crass and calculating villains in public, and then go and dine quietly together and talk cricket. We even pay a salary to the leader of His Majesty's Opposition. But we have to face the fact that this political game cannot be played in the European theatre as a whole. Accusations are hurled, whether true or false, with the express purpose of inflaming public opinion. And they do inflame it. Men are not really talking humanly to one another, nor even to their own public. They are creating an impression for a precise purpose. It is not a debating society. It is not a court of law; for there is no accepted law to argue about. It is part of the technique of conquest. It is meant to conquer men's minds and emotions in the mass. It does so conquer them, and then the mass may move.

Can we resist this process? Yes, we can, but only by the most careful examination of acts and by an incessant vigilance of temper. Should we always resist it? This is perhaps the most difficult of all political decisions. An unscrupulous orator may yet be speaking a real truth. A man may have bad political manners and yet be inherently in the right. Are we to allow ourselves to be roused? Are we to be moved to what may be a truly righteous indignation? Are we to be afraid of our own social instincts? Can we stand by, cool and detached, while wrongs remain unrighted, however uncouthly that wrong may express itself? Is it possible to permit an evil to exist without in fact condoning it? That is the dilemma which faces the peacemaker, whether it be a man or a nation.

As society is organised to-day we cannot stand aside from the heat and dust of a national conflict without accepting at least the protection of that particular social life and order which the combatants are fighting to retain. We cannot follow our own personal affairs if these very affairs themselves exist only by virtue of the sacrifices of our fellow men. These are the thoughts which perplexed us twenty-five years ago. They are still unsolved, and they still harass us.

We as artists are in a peculiarly difficult position. Everything we live for depends on the safe provision of food, clothes, and houses to live in. It depends on the protection of a stable and ordered community. We live literally on the good will of our fellow men. If we ask them to be sympathetic to our needs and ideals, can we turn aside and ignore theirs? We may know as little of politics as they know of music. But we count on their sufferance in our own affairs. Can we refuse to help them in theirs?

I will not pursue the argument further. I said last September that it was our duty to pursue our own ideals unflinchingly for so long as the world we live in leaves us a detached corner in which we can work. If and when the world says it can spare us no longer, then we cannot be spared. I think we should not wish to be spared. We exist by virtue of a social order. If that social order is in danger, then our very foundations give way. We must therefore help to keep our social fabric firm, if we wish to preserve and practise those social arts which are its ultimate pride and adornment. We are citizens first, and then musicians, and we must accept the consequences of that destiny, its responsibilities as well as its privileges ...

... The war which has now descended on us may be long and ruinous, but the world will survive it, and if life as we conceive it is to be worth living at all, there must still be room in it for the things of the mind and spirit, and for the cleansing beauty of the arts. It is true that we must put first things first, and whatever task we are called upon to perform, for the preservation of our society and our social and national ideals, we must accept it unflinchingly, and bear our share of the public burden by service without limit. But until we are called to other duties, we may and should, I think, continue to fit ourselves for that vocation we here have chosen.

Twenty-five years ago, there broke on our nation, and on our College, what we still know as the Great War. You present students know of it only as history. We who were part of it are conscious of many differences between that outbreak and this. In the first place there was, twenty-five years ago, almost complete ignorance of what modern war means, and a large and bewildered minority was slow to understand the issues and implications which were involved in so vast a struggle. We began with the motto 'Business as usual.' For a time all the normal customs and activities of our nation went on. Many thousands of the more active spirits joined one or other of the fighting services immediately, and that flow of recruits swelled in volume until it gradually changed the whole structure of our society. It was not until 1916 that conscription was systematically applied to us all and the tragic waste and confusion of haphazard recruiting all too tardily cured.

To-day there is not a voice to be heard which doubts the justice of our aims, and very few indeed who take any fundamental exception to the devotion of all our resources to bringing these aims to a worthy end, whatever the cost, and whatever the sacrifice. We all know only too well what war means now. Yet that knowledge seems to fortify rather than weaken the resolve of man not to be cowed, not to be enslaved. We demand a world in which faith, and intelligence, and beauty, can live, and men are again ready to die rather than forswear these things.

It is this knowledge of twenty-five years past, and this resolve not to see the world enslaved by brute force, which has formed our present will, and our present method of national organisation. To-day we begin with a nation enrolled. When our turn comes we shall be told where our duty lies and sent to do it. We are not left in any dilemma of doubt. The Government has made it quite clear that the education of the nation must go on, in every field, and that the young must be fitted for normal life before they are torn away, if they must be, to fight for and save the state.

We here, therefore, are to continue and complete our studies. If and when those studies must give way to a deeper call, we shall be summoned, and we shall obey. Meanwhile let us work as hard as we can. If there is other work you can do to help the nation, you will do it. Here and now you will be musicians, developing your talents for the service and healing of the nation's corporate mind and heart, and carrying the torch of beauty into what we hope may yet be a saner and better world.

It is no secret that our example here, in trying to continue our work as normally as possible, has led some other institutions, which had decided to close, to reconsider the position and re-open. I am sure this policy is right, and the response to it has been better than I had dared to hope. We have over a third of our normal numbers already, and we are growing daily, and when you remember how large a proportion of our students live far from London, these are most encouraging facts. All our normal studies and classes will go on. We shall have at least one full orchestra, and possibly the framework of a second. Some of our clerical staff are serving. So are some of our professors. Others have duties and live too far away to come. We have had to extemporize new time tables and new allotments of work. I ask you all to accept without question the arrangements that have been made for you. They have been decided carefully and deliberately ...

... A word about A.R.P.[2] The first difficulty is gas-masks. You must have them, and you must not leave them lying about. They will not be accepted in the cloak rooms. And see that your name is clearly written on the outside of the case.

Air-raid warnings will be communicated throughout the building by the clerical staff. You should then come down to the basement or sub-basement, where chairs are provided in the corridors. The

---

2. Air Raid Precautions

49

Head A.R.P. Warden for this district has seen our basements and approved them. They may be used as public shelters too, for a limited number of people.

You will find the corridors redecorated, and even the garden has been prepared for planting. In spite of the war, I do not regret that these improvements, and the other new amenities, have been carried out. Indeed I am glad we have got them done just in time. Life is going to be strange in many ways. It will be anxious, it may be dangerous, but we shall not lose anything, either in work or confidence, by having a clean and convenient building to live in. See that it remains as clean, as orderly, and as cheerful as you can make it.

Easter Term 1940

... in the progress of any art, there is a fundamental principle that one must never lose sight of. You must produce the art before anyone can appreciate it. You must write your book before anyone can read it. You must paint your picture before anyone can be moved by it. You must perfect your playing and singing before you can ask the public to listen to you. This means that any life devoted to an art is a venture, and a venture of faith. And it is just this element of challenge, of adventure, which is at the same time both dangerous and attractive. You would be surprised how often young strangers come to tell me that they have a safe job and a reasonable living, and they want to abandon both and become musicians. I tell them the brutal truth, that you must have outstanding talent, outstanding character, and great good fortune, to do well in a world so precarious as that of music. Most of them, to my great relief, think twice and go back to their useful, if less exciting, daily work. A few take the plunge, of these still fewer will succeed. Yet there will always be these daring spirits who are ready to forsake all and follow the fitful gleam of an artistic future. In a sense they are the salt of the earth, whether they win or lose.

These thoughts are not out of place to-day, because on the incomparably greater stage of the world's affairs thousands, millions of men and women are now making the bravest of all ventures of public faith. Many of our own boys have gone. Many will go. Most of them would have gone in any case, just as they did twenty-five years ago. They have nothing to gain. They have everything to lose. Yet it is just this certainty of loss of youth, of comfort, of a trade or profession, of home and normal ties, possibly of life itself, which can make war so tragically noble, whatever we may think of it in cold blood. It used to be said that war would stop because it does not pay. But surely that may be a complete misreading of men's minds and hearts. A war that pays is so despicable that every good mind revolts at the thought. But a war that does not, that cannot pay, a war where at best we must risk far more than we can possibly preserve, more than we can possibly replace, that is the fatality of these days. That is the tragedy. And yet it is also in itself a victory, a triumph of man's spirit over the more material aims of life.

It has been said that war will cease when you can take the glory out of it. That is possibly true. But how can you take the glory, the nobility, out of the risk, the pain, the selfless sacrifice which millions of men and women are offering to the world to-day? What of the Finns? Is there a soul among us who can resist the infection of such devotion, of such valour? And what of the dumb Russian peasant soldier who has been killed or frozen at the behest of an order or of a policy of which he knows nothing? You may say that men get the Government they deserve, that a cynical and grasping clique could not exercise such power without at least the tacit consent of the governed. But is that true? And even if it is true, does it make a simple soldier's sacrifice less tragic, less unselfish, less moving? Even if the sacrifice is in vain, or mistaken, or clearly wrong, does that resolve the tragedy, does that excuse the waste, does that relieve us of the insoluble problem of a man's readiness to stake his all, without thought of gain, for an end which he can see but dimly, if at all?

No, I believe we are as yet far from understanding the deeper springs of human motives and endeavours, and until we understand them we cannot guide them. Four months ago we were on the edge of a volcano. Those who know best say we are still there. This may or may not be true, but what certainly seems to be true is that the struggle will not be over quickly, or without long and arduous sacrifices. There will be successes, there will be exhaustion, sooner or later there will be peace. But there will be no permanent and world-wide peace until all men can find in the tasks and risks of peace a call for endurance, for hardship, for supreme adventure, such as to-day inspires their defence of their lands, their houses, their inheritance and ideals.

51

Meanwhile we are the fortunate ones, for we have work we love, a place to work in, a future to preserve. Our lads will endure and defend us, and the world they come back to will be the world we are making. Let us at least keep the torch alight, the fires aglow, that on their return they may yet feel that their sacrifice was not in vain, their art not a dream, their future sane and secure, so far as you and I can make it so.

Midsummer Term 1940

I am writing this address during the week before term begins, and that means that I have not the slightest certainty as to what our circumstances will be when I deliver it. I can tell you what happened yesterday and what we hope to do to-day, but to-morrow is beyond us all. We have had our usual A.R.C.M. examinations amid these incessant air-raids, and it has been astonishing how candidates and examiners alike have turned up ready and cheerful. Candidates have come from all over the country, knowing neither when they would get here nor when they would get back. Our clerical and domestic staffs have been beyond praise. Several have had to leave their damaged homes. Some have had to be on duty at night and then walk for miles to get here. Few have had a tolerable night's sleep. Yet they have not failed. I have been sleeping (or rather waking) here during the week, but whatever the pandemonium of these long nights of guns and bombs, soon after seven I hear the usual footsteps, the hum of the 'Hoover,' and then those pearly glissandos which are made by a duster on a keyboard. Food appears as usual, and of the same high quality. When the story of these days comes to be written, we shall have to record that what we counted twenty-five years ago as the special courage of the trenches: the steady bravery of men doing their normal duty under incessant danger and discomfort: this same courage has been shown in these last weeks by countless men, women and children who did not know, and do not yet realise, what superb soldiers they are.

And now for ourselves. Our policy is that of the nation, to do our work as normally as we can, to learn to live with our circumstances, whatever they are, and not to play into the enemy's hands by allowing danger or dislocation to confuse or discourage us. You will all have to be ready, resilient, cheerful. You will have to make your own time-tables and get to your lessons and classes as best you can. We are fortunate in having a building which is tolerably safe in emergency. We may be damaged, or we may not. We shall try to concentrate our work into short days, and mostly in the middle of the week. Do everything you can to make the work of the office and of your teachers as easy as possible.

We have produced a concert scheme for the term, and we hope to carry it out here in the theatre. We cannot take the responsibility of admitting large numbers of the public, but there will be tickets for you and your friends, and the basement shelters are near. We shall not normally cease work at a first 'warning.' Arrangements will be made to tell you if real danger seems imminent. As for moving about London during the 'alert' periods, you must use your own judgment. Those of us who have been here during the last fortnight have found that people are more and more inclined to go about their business as usual, unless there is an obvious fight or gunfire going on.

As for the future, it is no use even trying to see more than a day at a time. A year ago there were some who felt we should not re-open, but wait and see. A good many of my recent letters have appeared to suggest that we might wait and see now. I cannot agree. Neither is it possible to remove ourselves and our instruments and facilities elsewhere. We must therefore either carry on here as normally as possible or stop altogether. We shall carry on. And we shall not stop until either we are ordered to, or circumstances make it impossible for us to continue.

The future therefore, provided we suffer no serious material damage, depends on ourselves. There will be a Royal College of Music in being so long as we make it. And we are here to make it, and make it courageously and well. I need hardly tell you how glad and proud we are to see you all, here in London, which has now become a real battle front. And I need not stress our pride in all those past, recent and present members of our community who are serving the nation actively elsewhere. Lastly I want to give a special welcome to those new students who have braved the times and joined us. May we all live and work through these historic days, and to such good purpose that we may prove worthy of our special gifts. As we now share the risks of war, so we shall, I hope, earn the ultimate reward of peace. Whether that peace comes soon or late, may it find us still steadfast, still undaunted.

Since I last spoke to you, we have had our first direct experience of air-raid damage. An incendiary bomb pierced the roof of one of the Opera dressing-rooms. In that room nearly all our wardrobe was stored. Thanks to the efforts of our fire-fighters, heroically led by Mr. and Mrs. Devenish, the fire did not get beyond that one room. The night was pitch dark, the smoke was so dense in the Theatre and passages that it was almost impossible to grope through, and quite impossible to find anything once lost. The task of getting and handling buckets and pumps was a nightmare. We were helped by a squad from the Imperial College, who bravely entered unfamiliar rooms and passages, knowing neither what was in them nor where they led. By pouring water on the roof the fire was kept from bursting through, and the damage, apart from dirt and water, was confined to the wardrobe itself. Much was destroyed, including many historic and valuable costumes, but we shall save a good deal and gradually repair and clean what is left. On the whole we have every reason to be thankful. Apart from bruises and ruined clothes, no-one suffered hurt, and we can never be sufficiently grateful to those who saved us from what might have been a far greater disaster.

A few panes of glass broken by shrapnel is all that has happened apart from this fire. A fire-squad of students is on duty every night, and everything which courage and foresight can do will be quickly and effectively done.

Musically, and in spite of our much smaller numbers, I do not think the College was ever in better health. The average of talent is very high indeed, every student has clearly made the resolve not to be intimidated or side-tracked either by risk or uncertainty, and this spirit is reflected in the music they prepare and perform. Many tributes have been paid to the quality and atmosphere of our wartime concerts, and visitors to the College, without exception, feel that the place is alive with well-directed effort and unfailing confidence. This is as it should be. Whatever else this war has taught us, it has shown the power of the human spirit to rise above unparalleled dangers, to continue a daily task or serve a chosen ideal without fear and without complaint, whatever the material hazards of life may be.

And now I should like to say a few words on matters which only indirectly concern this College, but which are worth recording in any chronicle of these times. The long dark nights and the very few facilities for entertainment have had their effect on our tastes and habits, and some of these effects have been decidedly good. Orchestral concerts, for example, have been crowded everywhere, and so have hundreds of smaller ventures of high quality. Whatever artistic losses we have suffered, and these are great indeed, we still have exhilarating evidence that there is a deep and permanent demand for the refreshment and recreation of spirit which the arts, and our own art in especial, can so well supply. This is part of that victory of the spirit which I have already mentioned.

In the field of literature, too, there have been noticeable gains. People are taking to books, and to good books, with a new ardour. Publishers and book-shops both tell the same tale. There is a large and persistent demand, not only for fiction, but for biography, history, science, poetry and plays. Many of you, I have no doubt, have lately been reading books which, in normal days, you might not have found time to know. And I hope that this habit will continue and grow. Nothing better helps to widen and ripen your powers as artists than a well-furnished mind.

I have certainly found immense interest and refreshment myself in some of the books that I have read in these days, and I want this morning to mention two, because they express in a most vivid way some of the values for which we as artists and musicians stand. One is Professor Dingle's 'Science and Human Experience' and the other is Miss Askwith's 'Life of Keats.'

It may seem strange that these two books should meet, yet they do, and so do many other apparently diverse avenues of thought. Fundamentally Professor Dingle is one of the growing number of scientists who never forget that what we call the scientific approach to the world is an abstraction, and sometimes a very narrow abstraction at that. He gives a striking example by quoting the first lines of Omar Khayyam, beginning:

'Awake, for morning in the Bowl of Night,
Has flung the stone which puts the Stars to flight.
And lo! the Hunter of the East has caught
The Sultan's turret in a noose of Light.'

Science, he says, challenged to express such a thought, would have to discuss the wave-theory of light, the analysis of prismatic colours, and produce terrifying mathematical formulae of quanta and wavelengths and heaven knows what. In this process the actual experience to be described, which is a sunrise, and all that a sunrise means to our minds and imaginations, completely disappears.

You can apply this process exactly to music. The three or four chords, or the turn of a melody, which we call music, can only be described scientifically in a forbidding complication of vibrations and harmonics, and all the paraphernalia of mathematical acoustics. And when you have done all this the music, as music, is no longer there at all. The very process of abstraction is only possible by ignoring the actual fact, namely the musical experience itself, which you are trying to explain.

And this is where we come near to Keats. Keats lived in an intensity of spirit which wore him out even when he was in health, and which gives both to his verse and prose an almost blinding radiance of inspiration. And this intensity was what he called the overpowering sense of beauty, beauty of words and thoughts, beauty which at its highest is poetry. Until biology and psychology become much wider in their views, and much clearer in their terms, than seems likely for a long time, it will be impossible even to attempt to analyse what was for Keats the one surpassing value in life. It is certainly useless to talk about brain-cells or glands or whatever may be the physical apparatus of thought. The more you analyse in this way, the more completely the essential experience evaporates. And it is mere word-spinning to suggest that wave-particles, or resultant tones or ductless glands are more 'real' than our experience of a sunset, or a melody, or a poem.

There is a wide field in the world for scientific analysis and all that it implies. No-one would challenge that. But it does not and cannot yet touch the world of aesthetic values in which painters and musicians and poets must live. And it is important to-day to stress this fact. There has been far too much intellectualisation of the arts in recent years. Too many of the fashions and systems and 'isms' of various kinds, which have infected so many aberrations of the arts, have been founded on some theory or abstraction which ingenuity has spun out of its own head. People play music, and write about music, and even compose music, who do not seem to feel music at all. Yet music is fundamentally an aesthetic experience, not a scientific one. The intellect is there to discipline and control, but it can never be of itself the basis of an art.

I must not go further into these deep waters. What in essence I want to say is that we here are concerned with certain fundamental artistic values. They are values of experience. They are actual, they are real. They are not to be expressed in any other terms than those of music itself. And only those of us who have a faculty for intense musical experience, and who can convey something of that quality into the music which we ourselves play or sing or write, can hope to preserve and maintain the heritage on which all true musicanship must be built.

September 1941

... I am constantly being asked, when I try to advise students as to the choice before them, and the effect of war service on their future plans: 'Oh, but shan't I lose all my technique? Shan't I have to begin again? Shall I ever make up the lee-way? Shall I ever recover the skill I have managed so far to attain?'

I will give you a general answer to these questions, and two illustrations. The general answer is this. You do not play music with your fingers; you play with your head, with your intelligence, your character, your sensitiveness. Practising an art is only in a very secondary sense a physical process. You can practice mechanically all day and learn nothing. The quality of your work depends not on your muscles, but on your brains. To play really well your whole personality has to be tuned and tempered, receptive and sensitive, resilient and experienced, alert and vital, poised and concentrated. And the effect of being flung into new circumstances, of living through vivid events, of absorbing changed surroundings, always provided that you come to no permanent physical harm, can be such a tonic, such a stimulus to your whole character, that you may well become a more genuine artist than ever before.

The greatest artists in the world are those who have felt most intensely and absorbed most deeply the impacts and chances of human experience as a whole. You do not become an artist by withdrawing from the world, but by widening your knowledge, your sympathy, and your consequent powers of understanding and interpretation. To be a complete artist you must be a complete and balanced person. Your initial talent may be your own, but the quality and character you clothe it with will depend on your ability to accept every experience and master it. That is my general answer. You will be all the better musician for being a willing helper in the defence of the world.

Of my two illustrations one is personal, but no worse for that, I hope. Like most of my contemporaries I left music in 1914, and I did not come back to it finally until 1921, an interval of over six years. I will not describe the varied events of those years. Somebody has well said that soldiering consists of long periods of complete boredom varied by short periods of complete panic. In 1918 I was suddenly asked to give an organ recital. I had not played the organ for four years, but in a couple of hours I felt as competent as ever, and I got through my programme from memory without feeling seriously worried at all. And when at last I came back to music in 1921 I returned with a freshness and keenness of which something, I hope, still remains.

I was reminded of these facts the other day, when one of the most brilliant of our recent students called to see me. He had been in the army for 18 months, had not played seriously for over a year, and had then been asked to give a recital. He repeated exactly what I had found myself twenty years ago. He played as well as ever, and practically without any preparation. He was, of course, superbly fit physically and temperamentally, and under those conditions all his talent was at its highest pitch. That is the secret of the finest achievement; not routine, but sheer fitness and intensity.

Don't worry, therefore, about your immediate chances. There is no safety anywhere to-day. While you are here work hard. If you have to go and do something else, face it cheerfully and do it with all your might. When you come back you may well find that you have not lost but gained. For the gain of an enhanced appreciation, and the power to endure and surmount the hard knocks of life, may give your talent a quality and a certainty which nothing can defeat. You will be a graduate of that best of all schools, the school of experience.

Last term a group of students asked me to talk to them about musical careers in general, and more particularly about the best ways of finding a first suitable opening for professional work. I tried to describe the circumstances that you will all meet when your student days are over, and I gave examples of how past students had, from very small beginnings, eventually made good. I think it may be helpful if I repeat briefly what I said then and add a few further comments.

The dislocation of the war has of course destroyed many of the enterprises that gave work to musicians, and the whole basis of a musical career is at present fluid and uncertain. But even now there is necessary and important musical work to be done, and sooner or later we shall have a new and active future to face. What I have to say, therefore, will apply to some extent to present conditions, but still more to that recovery and expansion in which you will ultimately have to take a share.

Now in considering a professional career of any kind there are two main factors, the chances that are offered and the people who apply for them. These people are yourselves, and I want to discuss the subject to-day by outlining the various categories into which gifted music students can be divided.

Students in a College like this are roughly of three types. There are first the few whose talent is so outstanding that with reasonably good fortune they will succeed well by sheer individual distinction. Even in this select class, however, qualities of character and concentration are just as important as talent, great though this last may be. Take the solo performer as an example. There is not to-day, and there never has been, more than a handful of artists who could live by concert engagements alone. And there are still fewer who can do this from the beginning. If you wish to be a solo performer you will have to seize every chance that comes, however humble or unpromising, and you will have to play or sing with unfailing mastery, however small the audience or the pay. Nobody is going to buy tickets, and therefore nobody is going to pay good fees, for an unknown performer, and you can only become known by constantly giving fine performances, at first for small fees or none.

Young solo performers are like young barristers, who must take a brief for nothing rather than sit idle. Otherwise no-one will ever discover their talent at all. When a young barrister defends some penniless defendant skilfully, there is always a solicitor in the court who says: 'That's a promising young man. I must remember him.' That is the way all the great advocates have begun. That is the way you will have to begin.

The second and by far the most numerous class of student includes all those who will become free-lance chamber music or orchestral players, accompanists, organists, music masters or mistresses, and the best private teachers. One cannot draw any strict line between some of these and some of the solo performers, but there is a broad distinction between their aims. Nor can we always place any student permanently in one category. Some have precocious ability which never seems to get any further. Others develop late and rise to unexpected heights.

It is this large second class, however, which is mainly responsible for the general standard of practical music in the country. Their first opportunities may not appear to be very exciting, but they are solid and varied. In this field you must have talent, but you must above all have resolution and steadiness. Nowadays the orchestral player has to be something of a virtuoso to enter a good orchestra at all. The rest is hard work and genuine keenness. You must take anything that comes and prove that you are worth that and better. Orchestral leaders do not begin at the front desk. They have to earn their promotion. And the day is long gone when any scratch party of players could make a good ensemble. Success in these fields means unfailing reliability and unremitting work. The same is true of pianists and accompanists. Accompanying is now a highly specialised task, and the plums are few. But there is room at the top, and many an accompanist has become, by working with fine soloists, an expert coach, teacher, or conductor. The organist has to play well, but he has also to learn to handle choirs and congregations. He becomes as it were an institution, and if he has also a flair for conducting he will find amateurs in the first place, and later perhaps professionals, who are glad to play under his direction. He is often the centre and guiding spirit of a whole neighbourhood, directing excellent musical enterprises of all kinds.

Then there are the music staffs of Colleges and Schools. For the best of these you must be able to play well, to teach well, and to infect others with your skill and enthusiasm. And, lastly there is the large field of the good private teachers. It is a great mistake to imagine that there is something dull and unattractive in teaching as such. It is a highly skilled profession, and there are very few professional musicians who do not sooner or later make teaching one of their main activities.

Actually most of our enterprising students combine all kinds of work when they first have to make a living. They play or sing solos if the chance comes, and they may be among the few who so convince the world of their special talent that they graduate into the small class of pure soloists. Many more combine free-lance ensemble or orchestral playing with a little private teaching or a part-time school post. Singers may in the same way get bread and butter from a professional choir or chorus, while they feel their way to solo engagements and perhaps teach a little as well. Those musicians who go into Colleges and Schools have a fixed life's work before them, if they make themselves worth the best permanent posts. There is really no limit to the work and opportunities that may arise in this sphere.

In all these varied fields there is one invariable rule. Your professors and friends may be able to give you a first chance. They cannot keep you in a post or push you into promotion. You have to earn that for yourself. The indispensable qualification for success is that you never fail to do your utmost in whatever work you have a chance to do.

If you look through the list of our most successful artists you will find that almost invariably their careers have been really self-made. If you don't sing well for one guinea you will never be offered ten. If you can't prove your worth in a scratch orchestra you will never be asked to lead a good one. If you can't make music with a suburban choir you will never be given a cathedral or a big choral society. If you can't interest average pupils and make them efficient and keen you will never be given those of remarkable talent. All this may sound hard, but it is the simple truth. 'The race is to the swift, the battle to the strong.' If you are not holding your place, do not rail at Providence. Examine yourself and find out what you lack, either in skill or devotion.

For remember you have one reward which is great and rare in this world. You are working at the art which you have yourselves chosen. I remember years ago, when I gave a cheque to a young quartet that I had been able to engage for a concert, one of them said: 'Fancy being *paid* to do what I like best in all the world!' That is the infecting spirit which can make of an art at the same time an absorbing passion and a happy livelihood.

Finally there is a third class, consisting of those students who for various reasons will not enter the professional field. England is full of accomplished amateurs who have had professional training but have found other occupations or ceased to work professionally at all. They are the backbone of countless amateur organisations. They keep alive an enlightened interest in music wherever they live. They and their friends are the cream of the audiences which support all the good music there is. Directly or indirectly they do more than any other class to provide opportunity and encouragement for the professional. They are the kernel of our musical public, and we should be in sad straits without them.

That is a broad picture of our musical world, from the aspiring student's point of view. It is in that world and under those circumstances that you will all have to make your way, whether in war-time or peace-time. Three qualities are essential to you all. Talent, character and good fortune. Good fortune may lie in the chances that we and others try to give you. Your future then depends on your own skill and on your own integrity.

I am afraid this address has become rather a sermon, and sermons are not fashionable to-day. But it is no use pretending that the way of the artist is easy, and what I am preaching is the experience of all who have achieved any degree of success. Some people can give sound advice, some can take it. Let us hope that in this College we can do both.

Summer Term 1942

The other day I came across a quotation from Goethe, a thought which has been expressed many times and in many ages, but which remains perennially true. Goethe's line is this: 'Es bildet ein Talent sich in der Stille.' One may fairly translate it into 'talent grows quietly' or 'talent grows in tranquillity.' And as we are here particularly concerned with special talents, and our whole purpose is to foster and develop them, we must contrive somehow to apply Goethe's maxim to ourselves, even in these exceptionally turbulent and hazardous days.

Goethe contrasted this thought with another equally striking one. He goes on to say that, whereas talent needs quietude, character grows best in the stress of circumstances, in what he calls the stream of events, the changes and chances of life. No one will pretend, I think, that we to-day are not getting our fair share of changes and chances. If risk and danger and anxiety are good for our characters, then I think we are being given a generous education. We ought not to fail on that score.

You have heard me say on various occasions that to be a successful artist one must have at least three gifts, talent, character and good fortune. Good fortune we cannot control; character we can exercise daily in the rough and tumble of social life. There remains the problem of our talents, of educating them gradually and steadily and quietly. It seems almost a mockery to tell young people to-day that they must work calmly, without heat and without fuss, in spite of the earthquakes, both social and physical, in which we have to live. None of us can escape, nor should we if we could, the upheavals of a universal war. And our struggles will not end even when peace returns. Everyone of us, for the whole of our lives, will have to face new and urgent problems. We can no more go back twenty years than we can go back two hundred.

What then of our talents? Where are we to find that calm, that poise, that quiet development, which a proper growth is said to need? Where in the volcano of war are we to find solid ground? How amid the stresses of a new social order are we to preserve and pursue an unruffled constancy of purpose?

Now the first thing I want to say about this ideal of quietude is that it is not external, but internal. It is a quietude of spirit, a calm of set purpose, a poise and balance of mind and heart. It is inside the artist, not outside. We live in difficult days, but so did classical Greece, and mediaeval Italy, and Tudor England, and revolutionary Europe. Yet in these turbulent states and turbulent periods much of the finest art of all time was produced. So remarkable is this coincidence that some historians have felt driven to the belief that civil or national disturbances appear to be almost a condition of artistic vigour. Time after time we find genius producing its finest fruits in the midst of national, social, or intellectual convulsions. How are we to account for this, and yet accept Goethe's maxim?

Many years ago I worked in a public school where 120 boys of round about 16 years of age lived in one very large room. They did not sleep there, but they had no other place in which to spend their own time. They worked or played there, raged, shouted and sang, brewed tea, cooked sausages, scrambled for cups, knives and jam-pots, and altogether turned the place into the liveliest pandemonium I have ever seen. Yet one of my pupils used to sit in a corner of that room and paint pictures, write poems and set them to music, as if the surrounding hullabaloo simply did not exist. He might have been sitting in quiet solitude for all the effect the place seemed to have on him. He just retired at will into a calm of his own making, which nothing short of direct physical violence could destroy. He became later a good soldier, and later still a distinguished scholar.

That is an extreme example of developing a talent in deliberate detachment. It is the artist's state of mind which matters, not necessarily the hurly-burly in which he may have to live. And in some ways the greater the turmoil outside the more he is compelled to guard and cultivate a power of internal concentration, of calm purpose, of unwavering attention to his work. It may well be the very uncertainty and restlessness of life which challenges an artist or a thinker to preserve his balance, retain his sensitiveness, make and keep a quiet corner in his own soul. And it may well be that social and political disturbances do in fact cause such a severe winnowing, as it were, of the less gifted spirits, that only those of supreme quality and iron control survive in history.

We cannot all be of this highest class, but we can all to some degree cultivate a power of concentration, an attention to essentials, a detachment from the more shallow distractions which surround us. We can retire from time to time into the citadel of our own art.

The word 'escape' is to-day somewhat tarnished. Men think of it as a running away from trouble or responsibility. And so it can be. If we escape into ourselves merely to avoid the truth, to fret about our own problems, to become self-centred, self-justifying, self-pitying, then we had far better stay outside and seek what distraction we can find. But every man who is devoted to a high task of any kind must be able to refresh and recreate himself by periods of repose, of contemplation, of detached and single-minded judgment of what he is trying to do, and what end he is serving. More than this, he should at times get completely outside preoccupation of every kind. He must go into his shell in order to emerge the stronger. He must sleep well in order to work well.

Some of the saddest and most complete failures in life arise from vain dreams and selfish illusions. This is one of the dangers of the lone furrow. When you seek or make that quietude of mind within which your talent is to grow, you should not be thinking of yourself at all, except in so far as you are the instrument through which something wider and greater than yourself may find expression. For us here this concentration of thought should be music, music and nothing else, least of all our own fads and fancies. This control does not at first come easily. And it should never be either vague or mechanical.

To take a very simple case, I am convinced that some students practise too much, or rather practise too superficially and for too long. Practice at its best is complete concentration focused towards a conscious musical ideal. It is intensely hard work and it demands the most intense and constant sensitiveness and attention. When you are too distracted or too tired to think and feel vividly, you are not fit for practice. Shorter hours and better work is the cure. And remember too that practice should itself be a relief, a tonic, an outlet for all those mental and emotional stresses which are the foundations of artistic life, which are at once its stimulus, its danger, and its triumph.

The triumphs of a performer are not made on the platform. They are made in those earlier processes of careful preparation which must be undeviating, undistracted and unhurried. It is in these periods of controlled and unruffled work that you must feed your talents. This is the only way in which you can fit yourself to encounter and surmount the sterner tests of public and artistic life. Talent needs quiet, and patience, and time, but once made secure and permanent, it need not fear the future. It then merges into that sustained fortitude and strength of purpose which is an indispensable condition of all genuine artistic achievement.

... I have recently read, more than once, Stephen Spender's little book called 'Life and the Poet.' It is one of the most stimulating discussions I know of the problem that besets all artists in times of political convulsion. How is poetry to live in an atmosphere which is apparently a denial of the values that poetry stands for? And what, indeed, are the actual values which belong specifically to poetry? Do they include political and economic man, as well as rejoicing or sorrowing man? Is the Stock Exchange a subject for poetry, or the Trades Union Congress? Or shall we sing about bullets and mechanical drills, as old poets sang of the flight of arrows and the hammer of Thor? Are modern weapons and tools less human than ancient weapons and tools? Is any particular experience of the human mind and will less poetical than any other experience? What is the poet to do? Is he to ignore, or select? Is he to praise, or blame? Is he to rush into the battle, or sit aloft and contemplate it? Many of these are not Spender's questions, but they are suggested by his theme. There are many clear problems. First, should a Jewish musician of great gifts, moved by the sufferings of the persecuted, enter the political arena to champion the oppressed, and thereby perhaps lose his music in the throes of a political struggle? Secondly, if he cleaves to his music, should it be deliberately tinged by a racial bias? Should he use his art consciously as propaganda? Should he choose such subjects as appear to have a national, or a political, or a social implication? Can he be a 'left-wing' musician, a 'right-wing' musician, or any other labelled instrument?

Again, is it not the function of the artist to preserve an ever-fresh, an ever-sensitive eye, to see everything that comes, and however often it comes, with undimmed creative magic? Forms and colours are to him never stale. Every glance, every image, is to him a picture. Nothing is beautiful in itself, nothing ugly, but as the mood of the artist makes it. There are no limits to subject-matter, and the greater the artist the wider his range. Is there any difference, viewed purely as a possible channel for an artist's genius, between a sunset and a slum?

Finally, can an artist live without some belief, some philosophy, concerning fundamental values? Are these values to be confined by particular circumstances or events? Are not all circumstances, all events, part of the pattern of life, and is not the artistic gift simply this, that it can transmute all the material appearances of the world into the living spiritual experiences of men? The artist takes words, or colours, or sounds, mere symbols in themselves, and he gives them artistic life. He translates the prose of statement into the poetry of inspiration. He must see clearly, he must feel intensely. But he is not arguing, he is not preaching, he is not even teaching, in any direct sense. He is just evoking in us all whatever spark we may possess of his own refining fire. He can never be greater than humanity, because that is his canvas. But neither should he be less than humanity, in all its aspects, for anything less is a restriction, a narrowness, a distortion.

These are hard words, because some of the circumstances of life may be well-nigh unbearable. That is why great poets have written great tragedies. They have tried to understand the crimes and follies of men and dissolve them into pity, and sympathy, and hope. They have also taken the ordinary pleasures of life and turned them into rapture, and contentment, and peace. Yet it is a mistake to suppose that we in these days are tried more sorely, as individuals, than were men and women of the past. There has always been danger in the world, and uncertainty, and ill fortune. It is the province of the artist to create, by his sympathy and sensitiveness, a solvent for the daily cares, and a language for the unspoken joys, of all men in all ages.

And that, however small we may be by comparison with the great, is our function here. The humblest student who is genuinely and whole-heartedly following the artistic path is one of the great company of musicians. We all belong to that army whose leaders wrote and played and sung, and are now writing and playing and singing, the music which is at the same time our own heritage and our own living profession of faith. If we can do no more than guide the talent of a child, or accompany a musical friend, or play in a little concert, we are none the less part of the great musical world which inspires and comforts and draws together all the myriad hearts which respond to music. Some of us can do more, some less. It is quality that counts, not quantity. There can be a finer impulse in a simple song well sung, than in a welter of orchestration that is merely clever.

And we live in a world, not of Albert Hall concerts only, but of music in schools, and factories, and village halls. It is indeed precisely this demand for music in the most varied places and circumstances which is so remarkable a feature of these days. There is not one student here who need be afraid that there is no place for his talent. It may not be among the greatest. What is far more important is that it be among the really genuine, the devoted, the team-workers, who are the salt of our musical earth. That is a contribution we can all make. Let us make it, and leave the rest to Providence.

Summer Term 1944

... The capacity for broad human sympathies is one of the chief ingredients of genuine artistic expression. There is no such thing as a merely personal art. All art is a give-and-take between those who have a special gift for expression and those who are ready to feel and understand that expression. No artist can really transcend his public. If he does not evoke in them some measure of sympathetic response he is a failure. And the range and depth of this response will depend on the range and depth of the artist's own sensitiveness. The miracle of Shakespeare is not only Shakespeare's personal genius, but the unique breadth and intensity of the human panorama which he could encompass, and which could in turn find its expression in his work.

Another lesson the war has taught us is that there can be a positive tonic in stress and danger. In 1939 everyone thought that if we were seriously bombed we should at once have thousands of people mentally and nervously wrecked. In fact the opposite happened. There has been less mental and nervous disease since the war than there was in peacetime. Danger and uncertainty drive one to the more basic things of life, not to one's own little complaints. There has been more heroism, more sympathy, more good-tempered fortitude in our most sorely tried people than anyone would have believed possible.

I was particularly conscious of all this on that night last term when we lost about 250 windows. It is true none of us was hurt, but it seemed absolutely impossible that we could open the building for the Monday's work two days later. Yet no sooner could the damage be seen in daylight than the staff and firewatchers in the building set to work to clear it up. In two days our own men had patched up 20 to 30 rooms, working all Saturday and Sunday. On the Monday itself no lesson had to be cancelled and two or three days later the whole building was habitable. I shall never forget that work or the men who did it. They provided one more proof that material hazards so often seem to call out all that is best in us. We forget our own personal concerns in the spontaneous determination not to be thwarted by circumstances, if it is humanly possible to overcome them.

You, when you go out into the world, will meet difficulties and hazards, not only those arising from the war, but all the disappointments and mishaps of a normal career. I hope you will face them, whatever they are, with the cool courage which men and women have shown toward the material losses and dangers of these present days. It will be by that test that your rank as artists and citizens will be tried. It will be by those values that the quality of your work and character will be judged. This is emphatically not a world for the fine-weather sailor. And whatever kind of peace war may eventually bring to us, it will need all the energy, all the talent, and all the character we can devote to it ...

Christmas Term 1944

When we dispersed for the holidays eight weeks ago, it really did seem doubtful whether we could hope to come back to anything like normal conditions this term. For the first time in the five years of the war we had been compelled to cancel concerts and rehearsals, because we simply could not take the risk of having large numbers of people in one place. While the intensive 'blitzes' of the past had left us fair relief by day, the 'flying-bombs' came at any hour, with very little warning, and with devastating blast and splintering. We had no choice but to keep ourselves dispersed as much as possible.

And now here we are all back again, and our building has no new scars. There may yet be air raids of this or other kinds, but the risk may not interfere with normal planning for a normal war-time term. And we have this further satisfaction, that the flying-bomb attack, grievous and tragic as it was to so many innocent sufferers, diverted to London at least a part of the enemy's ruthlessness and venom, which might otherwise have been directed to destroying our soldiers in France. Eight thousand of these missiles, flung at the beaches in Normandy, might have altered the situation there very seriously indeed. It was an important factor that the great target of London was here, to obsess the German mind and bemuddle his strategy.

And what breathless days of victory we have seen in these past eight weeks! The war is not over, but the pattern of its end is at least beginning to be clear, and we can now, for the first time in five years, look forward to the gradual return of a saner life, and to an eventual healing of some of the more grievous wounds of our nation and of our civilisation. Five years ago we decided, so far as this College was concerned, that we would carry on our work as best we could, so long as our building was habitable and our students and staff able and willing to come. We have been providentially spared any serious material damage, and even the most drastic calls of National Service have left us many talented young students and most of the older devoted members of our staff. We have preserved our framework, and when the relief of peace allows us to expand again, all the essentials for that expansion are intact ...

We have to-day a large number of new students, including a considerable group of most promising new scholars. All of you, as well as many of those who were here last year or longer, will stay with us, we hope, long enough to live through the change from war to peace. On your talents will largely depend the quality of the new activities that peace will bring. You may see the return of many who are away fighting for us, whose adventures and experiences have so profoundly interrupted careers that began with fine promise here. Some, alas! will not return. They will have bought our freedom with their lives. But those who do come back are going to be given the fairest chance of recuperation and reinstatement that it is in our power to bestow.

The coming world needs you all, past students, serving students, and present students. And I have no misgivings either as to your quality, or as to the demands on the quality which will be made by the world that is to be. Whatever changes may occur − and they will be great and far-reaching − in our social and economic life, they will intensify rather than diminish the habits of scientific production, of large-scale planning, of greater and greater organisation of national and international activities which the war has in many ways ruthlessly accelerated.

We were all born into an age of machines, and these machines are now unalterably the first necessities of our organised life. We live to-day, as we fight to-day, by mass-production, mass-communication, mass-suggestion. None of these things in itself is either good or evil, but all of them, as we know only too well, can be directed to good or to evil ends. And all of them tend to regard the individual as a mere cog in a vast and uncomprehended mechanism. More and more the growth of an individual character or an individual talent must take place, if at all, outside the routine of the factory or office. Man has not lost his creative and enterprising spirit, but he cannot exercise it adequately in nine out of ten of the occupations which are open to him.

By virtue of these same tendencies, we shall find ourselves with more and more leisure. We shall be more spoonfed. We shall be clothed, we shall be housed, we shall be taught, doctored, insured and pensioned, with no more personal effort than the filling in of a few forms. With the help of the machines and the organisation which the machines make possible, we can satisfy most of our material wants in shorter working hours than ever before. What are we going to do with the rest of our time?

In the middle ages – and, indeed, up to the 19th century – 'totalitarian' war was unthinkable. Nine men and women out of ten had to dig, or spin, or starve. Very few men could be spared either to make weapons or use them. We have vanquished most of that manual toil. How are we to use the time we save? Are we going to find other fruitful outlets for the irrepressible energies of men?

We in this College are among the greatly favoured, for we have a profession which is absorbing, creative, and lifelong. Somehow we must persuade or encourage our fellow-men to find this or some other interest of a creative and satisfying kind, to fill their leisure hours and stimulate their leisure thoughts. This is really our mission, as I see it, whether our province be to create music, to interpret music, or to teach music. It is a duty we share with all artists, all craftsmen, of every nation and of every age. There is no peace in idleness, there is no peace in stagnation, there is no peace in suppression. Peace, whether in the individual or the nation, is a very delicate balance between a satisfying use of our own lives, and a sympathetic consciousness of the lives of others.

We must have a religion of values, human and individual, as well as national and social. And we must find expression for these values, both singly as men and women, and corporately as societies. Is not this precisely the purpose which the arts should serve, and especially our own art of music?

May 1946

Last term I spoke to you about some of the careers that await qualified students when they leave us. I dealt in the main with two broad categories. The first is educational, beginning with individual teaching and ranging through the whole wide sphere of schools and colleges up to important administrative posts under these or other authorities. This field also includes, at various stages, the control and training of amateur choirs and orchestras, both institutional and independent, and a great deal of concerted music of all kinds. This is the ladder that many of our old students have climbed.

The other broad category concerns more exclusively the executive ability of the performer as such, and ranges through orchestral playing to chamber music, includes accompanying and the very varied functions of the organist, and culminates in the few who can live on solo performances alone, either as players or singers.

To-day I should like to say something of the conditions that await you when you first have to rely on your own qualifications and qualities. And first let me stress the point that though recommendations and diplomas may give you your first professional work, they won't keep you in it, and they won't promote you to better things. Once you are launched on a professional career you will only succeed by the quality of your own work. Neither degrees, nor distinguished teachers, nor the hallmark of this or any other College, will do more than give you a trial run. From that time on, people will care little about your record as a student. They will observe your unaided and independent work, and judge you by that. Teachers succeed not by the certificates they hold, but by the solid competence or infectious artistry they can evoke from their pupils. The teacher is tested by the pupil.

This is especially true in schools and colleges, though here there are additional considerations of vital importance. If you are in a community you must be a part of it, and not an isolated and narrow specialist. You will have a headmaster or headmistress. I could write a book about headmasters. I have served under many, from the tone-deaf to the accomplished amateur. Oddly enough, in my experience, the purely musical qualities of headmasters have mattered little. What matters is the Head's attitude to education in general, whether or not his ideals are generous and wide. And this to some extent depends on you. You cannot expect special favours for your own department unless you also show a reasonable concern for the claims of others. If you work for the school as a whole, the school will work for you. That was my experience. Above all, you must learn to understand your colleagues and genuinely appreciate their varied points of view. Your aim should be to secure willing co-operation, not grudging acquiescence. Time and tact will accomplish much more than special pleading. Under every circumstance and condition you must be first-rate at your own job. That will bring respect, and respect brings approval, and approval may grow to active help in your direction.

All educational work, whether in school, or church, or club, or society, is essentially corporate, and you can never make a success of it unless your social sense is at least as acute as your knowledge of your own subject. Your results will depend on the response you can inspire, and that response will depend very largely on your instinctive appreciation of minds and characters other than your own. No one should attempt corporate or institutional music without such knowledge and sympathy.

The specialist performer faces different problems. He has to be to some extent self-centred. At its best his is an art of presentation. At its worst it is showmanship. But good or bad, it must be individual, and it suffers from the temptations of any self-regarding pursuit. In an orchestra the team work is both an opportunity and a safeguard, and the player who aspires to be a leader must show quite outstanding qualities. He must be a forcible and impeccable player, with powers of discipline both over himself and others. He must earn and deserve the loyalty of his colleagues. He must bear with a smile both the virtues and vices of his conductors. If the orchestra plays well, the conductor may snatch all the credit. If it plays badly, the players may have to take all the blame. That is the luck of the game, but in a good team it is a good life.

Chamber music is a class by itself, for here everyone is both a solo individual and a co-operating fellow member. Superb personal skill must be combined with consummate sensitiveness to the nature of the work and of the other artists engaged in it. It is probably the most ideally satisfactory of all forms of professional music, and the world needs more of it.

The solo performer proper, singer or player, may win unique laurels, but he will have to take many hard knocks. He stands up to be shot at, and he must take the consequences. He is the butt of criticism, public and private. He must neither get a swelled head nor wilt with despondency. He needs that very rare quality, a skin that is both sensitive and thick. He must learn to take Press notices, if he gets any, with a sense of proportion, even with a sense of humour.

A critic once wrote something like this: 'Miss So-and-So must be well known, there were so few people at her recital. However, she is certainly improving, and has already progressed from worse to bad.' If you aspire to be a soloist of real distinction, read that and keep smiling. There is only one thing worse than a bad notice, and that is to have none at all. And there is only one way to transcend all notices, good or bad, and that is to perform better and better every time, with unremitting study and preparation, and unfailing concentration on the best of which you are capable. Never mind if a critic says you sang too fast when it was, in fact, the conductor who drove you relentlessly. Never mind if something or somebody spoils what you intended to be a most convincing phrase. Try again next time, go on trying, aiming always to be better poised, more sure. Listen to yourself, listen to others, and try to put the best you can learn into everything you do. The life of the soloist is often hard and precarious, but it has its compensation when the youngster, beginning from nothing, eventually reaches acknowledged rank, neither too elated nor too worn out by the process.

One thing is true of both these fields that I have been describing, the educational one of fostering talent in others, and the executive one of developing one's own quality of performance. There is no end to either process. Of few professions can it so truthfully be said that we can go on both learning and enjoying from the cradle to the grave. This is partly due to the fact that most of us touch both sides of our art, the educational as well as the personal. We begin as pupils and our early career usually leans to the performing and executive side. As we grow older – and this is true of even the greatest performers – we begin to feel the desire to pass on our ideals to others and we grow to be teachers in some form or another. Finally, as our own executive powers begin to wane, we are drawn more and more to helping and encouraging those who are to follow us. This is a quite natural process, and it describes the careers of thousands of musicians of every race and rank.

I can wish you nothing better than that some such prospect should be yours also.

January 1949

... We have lost, without a moment's warning, Dr. R. O. Morris. He was examining here, during the whole of his last day, and within a few hours of leaving us he died. His achievement was a remarkable one, because there is hardly a place in the world, where music is taught, that does not acknowledge the authority of his text-books, and particularly the unique quality of his first book on sixteenth century counterpoint. We shall all miss him sadly, alike as teacher, colleague and friend, and I want this morning to recall that quality of mind which enabled him so to impress the world through the comparatively few pages of a slender volume. It is a quality we should all endeavour to share.

The problem of theoretical training in music is not new. You will find upstairs in our library hundreds of books, covering more than three centuries of time, all purporting to provide rules and guides for students to follow. Some of these books are large folios of many volumes, containing hundreds of precepts and examples, all claiming to analyse and clarify the methods of the great masters, and all suggesting courses of study by which the arts of musical composition can be apprehended and acquired. The result of this long chain of authority is that formidable structure of academic harmony and counterpoint which became by tradition almost a sacred text. All serious students were expected to master it, every teacher quoted his own teacher, and so on back to the dim origins of the system. It was all very impressive, but the more detailed and logical it became, the less connection it appeared to have with music that was convincing and alive.

Now the great innovation which Dr. Morris led was due to the natural independence and vigour of his own mind. He said in effect: 'I wonder. Are we really following in the steps of the great masters, or are we not rather studying one theorist's idea of what a second theorist taught about what yet a third theorist thought concerning what these elusive masters are supposed to have done? Let us avoid all this long chain of theory and deduction, and observe at first hand what the sixteenth century itself actually wrote, irrespective of any preconceived system, whether logical or not, whether according to rule or not, whether based on some recognisable form or on the unpredictable intuitions of temperament and genius.'

This was the foundation of Dr. Morris's epoch-making book, and it led him, and all subsequent writers, back to the real sources of our music. He abandoned a system, but he recovered a style. You cannot reduce music to rules, but you can learn to appreciate what is appropriate to a given period or place. There is no conceivable rule which has not been broken to good effect, but there is yet an underlying consistency of style which a sensitive student can recognise, and which will tell him what is apt and what is incongruous. Steep yourself in the actual music of a particular composer or period, and you can develop a reliable response to its prevailing atmosphere. You may not be able to reproduce Palestrina's strokes of genius, but you can become a tolerable exponent of his technique. Yet the more intimately you know the music the less will you be tempted to reduce it to rules.

This fundamental divergence between art and logic is within the experience of us all. No man has ever been clever enough or silly enough to try to reduce Shakespeare to rules, and yet anyone sufficiently familiar with his plays can say with fair confidence which features of them are indubitably his. Similarly you may say, if you know your Bach sufficiently well: 'This is, or is not, a Bach Fugue,' though no convincing description of a Bach Fugue is possible. Indeed, it is precisely this impossibility of analysis which marks the best examples. The more closely you dissect one of the forty-eight, the further away are you from the other forty-seven. If someone announced the discovery of an unknown Haydn Symphony, or Mozart Concerto, or Beethoven Sonata, none of us could give an intelligible description of it, because the very features that might stamp it as Haydn or Mozart or Beethoven are just those elements which are original, and therefore unique. You cannot classify convincingly even so simple a form as a Haydn Minuet, because no two of them agree in detail. And when we reach the more subtle elements of inflection and atmosphere we are completely baffled. Analysing a song by Schubert is like analysing the beauty of a rose. Beauty is in the heart of the beholder, as music is in the heart of the listener. Neither has any reality in a descriptive catalogue.

And it follows that what we have to find in the music of any period is its characteristic mood, its expressive power, its beauty. Its structure may be intellectually interesting, but structure in itself is only the framework of an art, and the more we concentrate on this framework the less shall we capture the essence of the music itself. I have had many composition pupils, but I am thankful to say that I never pretended to be able to teach composition. The best that a teacher can do is to encourage an attitude of mind that is sensitive and observant, and all he can demand is such technical practice as may enable the pupil the better to express himself. From this point of view, academic harmony and counterpoint have their value, provided one recognises them frankly for what they are, a very conventional set of musical tools by which a beginner may well sharpen his incipient musical skill. But academic exercises should always be accompanied by careful study of the style of a chosen period, and this can only be done by first-hand acquaintance with appropriate models. A pupil must develop his own power of discrimination. Neither teachers nor textbooks can do this for him.

And we may carry these ideas even further. Most people would admit that composition cannot be taught. But neither can playing or singing, in any really creative sense. It is the pupil who must play or sing, instinctively. No teacher can create this faculty. A teacher may demonstrate what players and singers have intuitively discovered in the past. We can provide good models, as it were. But we can neither manufacture the power to appreciate them, nor evoke any adequate response, unless the pupil has spontaneous gifts of his own. That is why a talented pupil seems to learn almost without being taught. What he hears, either from a teacher or from some other performer, appears to strike an immediate spark in his own latent fire, and he seems to achieve mastery by sudden revelation.

We are thus brought very near to the central mystery of the arts, and of all creative process. How does the seventh son, or the only child for that matter, of a village tradesman, become a great composer, or a great writer, or a great mathematician? Nothing can explain the miraculous powers of observation and memory which enable these exceptional beings to educate themselves by means of what appear to be totally inadequate resources. One of the greatest mathematicians of modern times was a Hindoo whose only teaching was derived from the elementary text-books of an obscure secondary school. These were enough to inspire processes of thought which led him to make astonishing discoveries. And I need not ask you who taught Mozart, or Schubert, or Chopin. They were not taught at all, as we humdrum people have to be taught. The slightest hint conveyed to an ear and mind of such sensitiveness discovers a genius that flashes immediately into achievements immeasurably greater than we can either emulate or explain. It is a sobering thought, particularly in a College like this, where we can provide every facility for learning, yet cannot create one spark of genius, teach we never so well and wisely.

For all I know, there is sitting before me now in this hall a young musician who in days to come will make a unique place for himself in the world of music. If he does, I hope he will remember this College with affection, though we shall, perhaps, owe more to him than he will owe to us. On the other hand, there may be no such genius among us. Whether there be or not, we all have our own portion of talent, and must make the best of it. That is the function of such an institution as this. We cannot create genius, we can only rarely even discover it, but we can try to provide an atmosphere and an environment in which such talents as we possess, be they great or small, can find nurture and fulfilment.

September 1949

... If you look at the general artistic problem with an open mind, and with some knowledge of the past, you will soon discover that it is not the most opulent and easy-going periods which have produced the best things in our artistic heritage. Indeed, one might almost say that without struggle and conflict, and the effort and discipline that these uncertainties and obstacles demand, there can be no real stimulus to endeavour, and therefore no victory of mind over matter, of character over circumstance. There is something in the sheer resistance of a block of stone which stimulates the sculptor to hew it into a significant and expressive form. The stark determination to master a technique is itself a part of the artist's genius. Far more young talents have been spoiled by facility than by frustration. A musician must find bread and butter in order to work tolerably, but he will do better work on that plain fare than on unlimited champagne and oysters.

The basic fact is that the arts are products of the imagination, and an imagination sufficiently vivid will triumph over almost any conceivable material circumstance. Think of Bunyan in Bedford jail. Think of the blind Milton and the deaf Beethoven. And there have been many less extreme examples where whole communities seem to have been stimulated, rather than discouraged, by the risks of a hard or precarious way of life.

From the purely artistic angle it is significant that in some of what we now call the greatest periods of musical history the actual material means available to the artist seem so poor and inadequate in comparison with the masterpieces he was then creating. We talk about our Tudor ancestors sitting round a table singing madrigals. It is a very pretty picture. But they were amateurs singing from single parts without tempi or expression marks or bar lines, and so far as we know without a score or a conductor. And when a voice was absent they played the part on a viol, or vice versa. What can it have been like, in actual sound?

The case of Bach is similar. He himself said he was well content if one performer in each part could read well. He never had more than a mixed company of fifty to sixty singers and players in all, and yet he hazarded with these the double choruses and orchestras and the most exacting and complicated texture that any musician has ever conceived.

Even the great Viennese period of Haydn, Mozart and Beethoven presents the same kind of enigma. The famous orchestra at Mannheim, which so impressed Mozart, was considered unique in its observance of marks of expression, but the wood-wind instruments were never in tune. It was, in fact, physically impossible to play consistently in tune on these instruments until a more modern mechanism was devised. Beethoven would never have heard, even if his own hearing had been perfect, even a tolerable performance, by our standards, of the greater works of his maturity. He, like his predecessors, wrote from his imagination. The music was created in his mind, and nowhere else.

And there was a political and economic background to the life of Beethoven not unlike the upheavals of our present days. Napoleon's armies were marching about Europe, governments and dynasties were falling, commerce ruined, social standards in flux. War left in its train devastation, disease, poverty and unrest. And yet it was in the very midst of these cataclysms that the great Viennese musicians, and our own great romantic poets, were born and had to live and face the world. Those of you who have read Ruskin will remember how he was driven to the conclusion that great art is the ultimate product of great issues, of great crises, of fundamental challenges to the spirit of men.

We to-day are being challenged by circumstances beyond control or prophecy. We must accept the fact that we live in an unstable and unpredictable world. But if history is any guide, it has often been precisely such uncertainties and dangers that have called forth the finest manifestations of human courage, steadfastness and faith. Our own immediate path is quite clear. Each of us is the custodian of his own small part in the march of truth and beauty, and the emancipation of our world will only come as each one of us loyally accepts and follows these ideals. We are greatly privileged because we are among the comparatively few people in the world who are allowed to devote their whole lives to a vocation they have themselves chosen. A musician may well be proud of his own art, but he should also be very humble in face of those who toil and spin that he may live. And he should be thankful if in return for this protection he can bring some measure of relief and refreshment to lives more dull or arduous than his own. That is his function in any civilisation, and especially in a civilisation so regimented and harassed as our own. Work

80

hard, therefore, and foster your special gifts, that you may perhaps help by your art to relieve some of the discords of the world. Nothing less than this can justify any of us in being here at all.

Music and the Church

In the centre of every European village there is a church. In nearly every town that can claim a few centuries of history, there is a cathedral. Scattered throughout our lands, sometimes in fertile valleys, sometimes in remote and forbidding wilds, are the impressive remains of great monasteries, once the most powerful communities, material as well as spiritual, which our world could show. These legacies of brick and stone, these columns and arches and towers, are the most striking relics of our past. Seen through the glass of history, they enshrine for us the major part of what our ancestors meant by civilization, by corporate devotion, and by the triumph of mind over matter. They stand, solid masses of masonry, as permanent memorials of the deepest and most persistent tendencies in the chequered fabric of our common story. They know no barriers of language. They have no political frontiers. Wherever Western civilization has found a lasting home, it has thus embodied its fundamental creeds. These buildings are milestones, magnificently impressive, along the road of man's spiritual pilgrimage.

Modern towns usually begin with a railway-station. This is not quite so stark a contrast as might appear at first sight. The railway now stands for that essential communication between man and his fellows which is the first bond of society. The road which preceded it also had its stations, and more often than not they were the village church, and the inn which proverbially neighboured it. Thence came and went the pedlars, the pack-horses, and the post-chaises which served our forefathers as the railway serves us. Their stages were from one village green to another, or from a cathedral square to a chain of hamlets. Their time signal, when time mattered, was the church bell, the cathedral chime.

The church itself was very much more than a house of devotion. It was a meeting-place and a refuge. There the lieges could gather, or the outlaws find a hiding-place. It was put to many kinds of social use. It was often a granary and sometimes a stable. It was a stage, not only by reason of the sacred Act of the Mass there displayed to the people, but also by less exalted portrayal of homely themes and incidents, often more sacred in name than in method, which unfolded crude but vivid truths and stories to a people to whom seeing and hearing were the only avenues of thought. The church was a concert-hall, and not for the adornment of a musical liturgy only. It housed all those tentative experiments in descriptive anthem and oratorio from which so much of our music, secular as well as sacred, is descended. The church was a council-chamber for the guilds of merchants and craftsmen. Not rarely it was an open market where goods were displayed, bartered, bought, or sold. It would be a very narrow view of history that should account these myriad churches of our countryside to be exclusively religious in their bygone use. Men were born, men married, and men died, and these elemental acts were given a communal significance and ceremonial long before common beliefs were formulated, long before any creed found a visible shrine. The Church ultimately took under its tutelage a host of customs and associations far older than itself. It then claimed, by adoption, a share in every corporate event which marked the lives of its children. Its children, in their turn, used the church for every social purpose. It was the one home of mankind in the mass. It was the one universal symbol of human brotherhood.

We have changed all this. We have sent our pedlars to the railway, our counsellors to the town hall, our merchants to their shops and markets, our millers to the elevator, our lenders and borrowers to the Stock Exchange, our actors to the theatre, our politicians to the club. That rich and varied pageant of all humanity which used to find its daily haunts within the walls or under the shadow of the church has not died. It lives and chaffers and gossips just as warmly and with just the same infinite variety as it did in the medieval church-porch. But it goes elsewhere. Our churches are lovingly cared for. They are far cleaner and quieter and more decorous than our ancestors would have deemed possible, or even desirable. We blush if we harbour a mundane thought in them. We tread slowly and silently and reverently. We make long journeys to admire their architecture, their stained glass, their monuments, their organs. We tremble to think what damage a profane hand or an ignorant taste might commit. Marvellously we protect, marvellously we restore. We preserve with meticulous care everything of historic or local significance; everything, that is, except the supreme historic fact that the church was once the unchallenged centre and meeting-place of the whole local community, busy men and idlers, rich and poor, old and young, traders, beggars, rogues, and lovers, men who worshipped and men who looked askance. Our consecrated gardens may now be trim, because the present world passes them by. Our cathedrals may be little more than the cherished museums of a life that is gone. A church can be very peaceful when it is empty.

There is loss as well as gain in all social changes. The church of the Middle Ages was much more than a symbol of religious faith. It was a great social institution, and it remained the most important channel of social influence for just so long as it found room for all sorts and conditions of men, in their workaday thoughts and habits. When we build pews in our nave, and close our chancel, we may improve the comfort and decorum of our worshippers, but we destroy those easier manners of the past which allowed men to go in and stand a while, or talk a while, or kneel a while, at any hour and on any day, when either business or leisure found them at the church-door.

We are about to devote a few pages to that splendid heritage of music which comes to us from the Church of the Middle Ages. It would be a profound mistake to think of this music as the fruit of a peculiar sect. Medieval music, like medieval architecture, was an outpouring of the whole spirit of man. Cathedrals were not built by great ecclesiastics, however noble their powers of inspiration and resource. Cathedrals were built by master-masons, designed, elaborated, and erected stone by stone at the hands of gifted crafts-men. No spiritual fervour will of itself teach a man even the begin-nings of an art. The music of the medieval church was written by musicians; by men, that is, of highly specialized technical gifts. Some were good men, some were bad men. Saints, knaves, and fools all had a hand in it. The Church could then find work for them all. Under no other conditions could an art so universal have been brought into being. For centuries Europe was amazingly rich in trained masons who were also great architects. She had also an inexhaustible supply of men so practised in music that no thoughts were too deep for its powers of expression. That all these gifts were so generously devoted to the Church was due to a relation of mutual understanding and respect. Artists portrayed the high aspirations of religious communion because the Church on her part provided a generous home for art.

It has often been debated whether there is in truth such a thing as religious art at all. There is good music and bad music, just as there are religious emotions of higher and lower order. These qualities can be combined in any degree. The scandalous masses written around ribald popular tunes, which sometimes were embarrassingly popular in the church, were often no less talented, no less inspired, than those which more carefully observed the proprieties. It is indeed doubtful whether, without a long succession of such daring and incongruous experiments, polyphonic music would ever have reached its ultimate perfection of method. Nature is prodigal of her gifts, but she is whimsical too, and cares nothing for our nice classifications. We have to hope that artists will be good men, or at least ready to work within the accepted ethics of their time. We demand so much of all men. But we do not expect a good man to be on that account an artist. That would be clearly absurd.

There have in fact been many of the great and good who saw in all forms of art at best a snare, at worst a vice. That has been one of the most persistent tenets of puritanism in all ages. The old prophets who broke down the carven images have found successors in every age and clime. St. Jerome and St. Francis eschewed the arts that they might not be distracted from a more mystical devotion. Savonarola and the image-breakers sought thereby to help men save their souls. There is no limit to the length to which these negations can be carried. There are religions where the very name of God must not be uttered, lest the pure thought of Him be in some measure narrowed or profaned. There are sects where men's portraits, either in paint or stone, are a sin, for God's image in man must not thus be counterfeited. Every society draws its puritan line somewhere. Some churches admit music, some do not. Some will encourage voices, but find instruments unseemly. There have been communities to whom the Campanile of Giotto in Florence and the west front of Rheims Cathedral were vicious influences, to whom the nobility of a spire, the beauty of an arch, the warmth of stained glass, and the subtle smell of incense were alike anathema. As for the grosser images of the heathen, there are two approved lines of attack. One is to smash the idols, the other to convert the idolater. It is of course far easier to break a statue than to change a man's heart, but both processes may be equally ignorant of artistic values.

And these restrictive sentiments may be as passionately defined and held among the devotees of a particular art as among the iconoclasts outside it. To some people music is rank emotion. It is a form of sentimental suggestion only to be welcomed when it stirs the pulse or melts the heart. If pulse or heart be of crude or uneducated type, then music may become a frank wallowing in primitive emotions. Others find such an appeal and such a product unbearable. They ask that the mind shall be engaged, as well as the heart; that the decencies of restraint, the canons of form, the resources of scholarship and craftsmanship shall not be overlooked. They would rather have no music at all than surrender their ideals of intelligent and conscious discrimination. Such conflicts of attitude can be traced throughout history, and can be plainly seen in all societies, great or small, which use or abuse the possibilities latent in all the arts. And the two main contrasts, as between intellect and emotion, are often curiously mixed. A sect which is extremely hard and uncompromising in its creed may have wild outbursts of enthusiasm of the most emotional type. Individuals can behave no less inconsistently. A life physically athletic and practical is often fringed with emotional responses that are very near the surface and very difficult to control. The lower deck is proverbially sentimental. At the other end of the social scale are the nimrods of the countryside, who in their semi-artistic accomplishments can be relied on to take the predominantly emotional view. Men and women who in their daily pursuits would blush to show undue feeling, will exhibit a taste in music or pictures or literature which is in fact an emotional relief for the sentiments they repress in other spheres. It was our most stolid middle class which sang with such fervour the more emotional of Hymns Ancient and Modern.

We can study these problems with unusual clarity in the arts which the Church has fostered, because we have there not only a long perspective of history, but also a tradition still largely preserved and showing the main influences of that past. Just as her stones are so often a representation of events long gone, so her liturgy gives us a panorama of the spiritual and intellectual epochs in her thought. A chosen hour spent in an English cathedral can teach us social and musical history more vividly than any treatise on these subjects.

The very walk through the avenue which leads to the church-porch may revive in us that ancient instinct which found a peculiar sense of mystery and solemnity in the dim glades of a northern forest. Countless generations of men have there been moved to awe and worship, and it is no accident which makes those stone forests of Gothic architecture, columns and arches and aisles, appeal so deeply to our religious sense. Under a southern sun men copy in their temples the protecting shadows of a great rock. Gothic architecture reproduces the majestic shelter of great trees. So deep are these associations that our respective civilizations find it almost impossible to think of religious architecture in any other forms.

The plan of our cathedral is equally embedded in historic truth. Look through the west door and you will see in the very far distance that high altar where only the supremely initiated may serve. These ministers face the east, whence came their teachers and prophets, but whence came also that earliest glow of the sun which was a sacred beacon before history began. Not so far, but still distant, is the screen which divides the ordered hierarchy of office-bearers from the mass of common folk. This plan is not only religious history, it is social and political history too. Call it King, Lords, and Commons. Call it bishops, priests, and penitents. It is all one, a moving embodiment of just those divisions and just those loyalties which for a thousand years and more were the very foundations of our state. Later and more protestant faiths have expressed other views. There are modern places of religious worship where organ and choir are arranged like the orchestra of a concert-hall. The congregation occupies an amphitheatre of unbroken rows. The seats are upholstered and the whole building well lit, heated, and ventilated. The minister is not unlike a president, the first citizen of a republic, as it were, standing in his central rostrum in full view of the whole body of political equals who have chosen him. We build as we believe. We paint, we write, we sing as we believe. We can do no other.

Listen to the sounds which come rolling down the great spaces of our cathedral nave. Here too are vivid traces of the past. The poise and dignity of a chanted monotone, the inflexions and cadences which mark, by a fall of the voice, the close of a phrase or sentence; these are the very beginnings of music. When men crystallize their corporate thoughts into a form of words, these words very soon become, by constant association, so well known that they are taken for granted, yet so charged with feeling that alteration is unthinkable. This happens now precisely as it happened in the infancy of the Church. Even those Protestants who have stood most firmly against mere conformity in religious worship find themselves insensibly acquiring a very different practice, but in the long run a no less liturgical one. It is a matter of use and wont, associated with deep feeling. There is a story of a local preacher who shocked his hearers by the invocation: 'O Lord, roll your shirt-sleeves up!' He should have said: 'Lay bare Thine arms.' Every society which puts its thoughts and feelings into a form of words develops a sharp sense of peculiar fitness, in secular as well as in sacred phrase. There is an unmistakably ritual form in some of our lightest pastimes. One must not alter or invent a descriptive term, even in playing a game. And once such a form has been fixed for its purpose and occasion it is a small step to give it a still more exact and ceremonial character by chanting. Nothing is more universal than this practice, in high and low civilizations alike. Repeat a significant word, and it becomes a cadence. A sentence becomes a chant, a chant a melody. To the stranger it may all sound like 'mumbo-jumbo'. To the initiate it is music. Hallowed by tradition and circumstance, it is sacred music.

When many voices chant together the words are lost, so far as clear articulation is concerned. Speech gradually changes into song. The practice of chanting the Psalms, universal in Western Christendom, could not have arisen except in communities intimately familiar with the words. A small choir may by careful practice chant so unanimously that the words can be spaced almost as naturally as in speech. But such singers are really singing from memory, for the hundredth time. It was thus that the psalmody gained so permanent a place in our religious music. The men who sat in the choirs of our abbeys and cathedrals a thousand years ago were going through an ordered sequence of religious offices day after day, month after month, year after year; and their predecessors had been chanting these same offices for hundreds of years before them. The Psalms themselves are of course far older than Christendom. It was the

Jewish origin of Christianity which brought the Psalms so naturally into the Christian liturgy, and it is probably to them that we owe the initial power and place of music in the early Church. For the words did not come alone. Many of the most ancient church melodies must be attributed in origin to the still older Hebrew music of pre-Christian times. The subject of origins so remote is difficult and uncertain, but of the two sources mainly available, Greek and Hebrew, the internal evidence points definitely towards the Hebrew. There is no such warmth of tone and expression in the few fragments of Greek music which we have been able to decipher. And in music of this elemental character, age and association are the most vital factors. The Psalms have both these features beyond all the other components of our liturgy. Our versicles and responses are mainly fragments of psalms. Our canticles are hymns and psalms of special or derived appropriateness. Words and music went hand in hand, and a thousand years of use brought to the early Middle Ages an art of church music of unsurpassed fitness and expression. This music fixed our intervals, our most constant melodic phrases, our cadences, and our earliest sense of melodic form. It was an art purged by devotion, serene by contemplation, warmed by communal tradition. Our music would have been something quite other than it is had not these centuries of choral use stamped it with the permanent seal of their long vocation, of their careful cloisterdom, of their essential brotherhood.

Two things defeat every historian, the slowness of time and the gradualness of change. We can record events, but we cannot record what appear to be the long and uneventful spaces between them. We cannot chronicle the thousand slight elements of a slow growth. For something like a thousand years our monasteries were the most permanent and powerful institutions in Christian Europe. The various orders arose at different times, and their aims and fortunes greatly varied, but the instinct to found and support these select and cloistered communities was one of the outstanding features of a very long period of history. Within these communities all the arts were at one time or another fostered and preserved, often to an exclusive and very high degree. A vast number of our present artistic legacies are derived from them. Of these our music is certainly one, and it is impossible either to understand or appreciate some of its main characteristics unless we can to some degree visualize the circumstances that gave it birth.

Plain-song or plain-chant, which was an advanced art of melody wedded to the Latin poetry or prose of the Church's liturgy, had already reached perfection a thousand years ago. It remains an unsurpassed type of musical expression. Artistic values do not depend on complicated methods or mechanism. These single strands of melody with which the hymns and psalms of the Church were adorned had a fitness and beauty which places them, simple as they are by later standards, among the highest forms of music which inspiration has yet devised. They remain still warm and tender, dignified and human, and they have been strong enough to bear an immense superstructure of more complicated ideas. Why indeed, it may be asked, were all these subsequent elaborations necessary, if a perfect art had already been found? The answer to that question would explain the mystery of all creative impulses. Men never have been content with their work, and the more gifted they are, the less will they be satisfied. These medieval communities were like ourselves. They solved one problem only to meet another. There is no finality in these things.

Slowly, uncertainly, and covering many generations of time, they began to feel their way towards the possible combination of one melody with another, towards what in the course of centuries became the art of harmony. Harmony is a unique product of our Western music. No other music in the world shows anything approaching it in range and organization. It has become the essential hall-mark of our musical sensibility. Other systems of music have made experiments, some have got so far as to combine various sounds to varying degrees. But as a system complete in itself, infinitely fertile, and supporting an ever-increasing structure of concerted music of all kinds, there is elsewhere nothing fairly comparable with the art of harmony as we know it. And there is no movement in artistic history more remarkable and more challenging than this urge towards elaboration and complexity of sound which busied the minds of European musicians for centuries. Roughly from A.D. 1000 to 1500 ecclesiastical music is a long series of experiments in harmony. The length of time and wealth of resource involved in this development are a fair measure both of the persistence of the impulse and of the sustained practice on which the final results were based. Practical trial and logical theory were both concerned with it, and their interactions are illuminating.

Medieval theories of music are not unlike medieval theories of astronomy. They began with a dogma, and if the facts of experience appeared to deny it, so much the worse for the facts. The circle is a perfect figure, therefore the planets must move in circles. That was the type of argument. Planets actually move in ellipses, and observation could have proved that then as now. But theory was much too powerful, and the sky had to be filled with intricate machinery in order that the obvious details of planetary movement should not destroy the theory of the perfect circle. In just the same way were musical theorists obsessed by figures. Octaves and fifths are perfect intervals, therefore harmony must reside in octaves and fifths. The fourth is an inverted fifth. Fourths were also perfect, and a harmony consisting of moving octaves, fifths, and fourths confronts us in all the early theories of the subject. In the matter of time-values the figure three had a special, even a theological, significance, and though men marched on two feet then as now, and their hearts gave alternately a stress and a relaxation, perfect time was held to be, not the physically universal rhythm of two beats, but the theoretical one of three. In the examples and discussions which have come down to us we can see this clear conflict between theory and practice. Art is not a system of thought, but an ordered method of action. Its proper field is that of trial and error. Musicians found themselves persistently inventing new sounds, hopelessly inconsistent in theory, but strangely moving in practice.

Naturally there was strong opposition, not only from the Puritans, who distrusted all elaborations, of whatever order, but also from those who pressed a theory, or felt acutely sensitive to the simpler values. Nothing we can say of our wildest contemporaries can exceed the condemnation visited on some of these medieval pioneers of harmony. 'This music defiles the service,' wrote John of Salisbury about 1150. Pope John XXII complains in 1322, nearly two centuries later, that music is 'depraved by descants, elaborations, flourishes'. Back to plain-song, octaves and fifths, is the cure prescribed. Meanwhile the bold spirits are preaching discords: thirds and sixths which 'make great melody'. Right or wrong, these 'discords' came

91

to stay, and some of them are the very essence of harmony as we know it. Children at play, like soldiers on the march, will add thirds to a tune by sheer instinct. No theory of intervals, however august, can prevail against the practice of them.

It was not all pure invention, or pure instinct. The echoes of a great building, by delay and deflexion of sound, must have accustomed men's ears to the combination of notes of considerable discordance. This may be one of the reasons why the device of Canon, where the same melody is sung by several voices beginning at different times, is so frequent a practice. It is also easier, on the path of harmonic invention, to have a known tune to hold fast. The writing of descants, where a more definite independence of parts is deliberately contrived, was a still more fruitful origin of new sounds. The results were often crude and clumsy, but from time to time there occurred a passage or a cadence so satisfying that it soon became part of all men's musical speech. Here too there was a known melody to hold to, in one of the parts. The other part performed the experiments. But given a beautiful, or even a tolerable, combination of two parts, why not three, or four, or five? Men's voices differ in pitch. Parts having different ranges of notes would be welcome on every ground. The whole extent of possible vocal sounds was gradually explored, and varieties of pitch were clothed in varieties of melody. Vocal polyphony learnt by slow degrees to find an effective, congenial, yet independent use for every type of voice, and the product was extraordinarily stimulating.

It offered an inexhaustible source of expression and adornment, and this was probably of all things the one which its promoters most eagerly craved. The achievement of harmony is unique in our story because the circumstances that evolved it were unique. Length and multiplicity of devotions was a fundamental rule of the great monastic orders. The daily round might include Matins at midnight, when the day began, Lauds at sunrise, Prime, Terce, Sext, and None at three-hour intervals, Vespers at sunset, and Compline to end the day. To these must be added the Masses which were celebrated in some communities almost without ceasing. Saints and Holy-days had their special rites. Many hours a day were normally spent in the Choir. The main outlines of the Liturgy were irrevocably fixed. Every office was sung or said times without number. Some rules included the whole of the Psalms each week. The Canticles and many of the Psalms were used everyday. The language of the Church was Latin, every syllable of it familiar, yet gradually ceasing to be a living language even among those most constantly called upon to use it. And this rule of life was the foundation of thousands of communities, great and small, rich and poor, of men and of women, for hundreds of years, and in every Christian land. Is it surprising that music, once it was admitted as a possible form of enhanced expression and embellishment, became one of the main outlets for that inherently creative impulse which no severity of negation or discipline can ever permanently quell?

These monks took vows of poverty, and every founder urged this renunciation with the utmost sincerity. But nothing could prevent the gifts of faithful or grateful worshippers. The monasteries were at first rude cells, such as the hermits of older times had chosen to inhabit. They found themselves unavoidably the possessors of steadily increasing resources. They became great capitalist societies, great patrons of the arts. The cells grew into vast piles of magnificent architecture, the garden plot into a great domain. In exact parallel a simple order of worship became an elaborately expressive ritual, and in this ritual was developed the most characteristic attribute of European music, the art of harmony. The simple responses which float down to us from the choir of our cathedral are relics of this music as the Middle Ages practised it. The steps in its evolution, Organum in perfect intervals, Canon employing one melody for more than one voice, Descant finding real melodic freedom in parts, can be studied in books and examples. So can the works of the greater pioneers, Dunstable, Dufay, Josquin des Prés, and their many fellow workers. The final result was a variety in unity, a many-voiced concordance, on which the whole marvellous wealth of sixteenth-century vocal music was built. These pioneers are in the main forgotten, but Palestrina knew them, and Lassus, and Tallis and Byrd and Gibbons. The whole order of society in which they lived and worked has gone, but the foundations of music had been well and truly laid.

All music is modern when it is written. Even a composer who is following no more than a traditional path finds something which, to him at least, is a new version of an old truth. Contemporary taste always feels that there is a peculiar fitness and satisfaction in the arts which it fosters, whatever the future may think of them. We have learnt to distinguish two main products of medieval church music which seem to us to represent perfection of expression within their respective spheres. Plain-song is a mature and finished art within its chosen limits. So is the polyphony of the sixteenth century. But had we lived anywhere in the intervening period of some five centuries, we should no doubt have felt every step in the development to be a culminating point in musical history. The first crude descants were, to those who devised and sang them, a last revelation of beauty, than which nothing finer could be imagined. Every age writes up to the limits of its vision, and the appeal of its music is deeply present and actual. It is we who find a simple plain-chant more satisfying than a clumsy experiment in harmony. The men who made the experiments had no doubt of their clear superiority over the methods of the past.

When, therefore, we extol the golden age of polyphonic vocal music, we have to remember that other ideals were already present and active, and those who embraced them were profoundly convinced of their fertility and beauty. Nor is the broad line of cleavage, between what we may call the music of the monastic church and those other forms of religious music which came later, merely an aesthetic divergence. It is a stark contrast between two distinct orders of society, between two ages which differed fundamentally in organization and vision. The atmosphere of serene contemplation which to our ears marks so much of the best music of the old liturgical composers was a natural counterpart of the cloistered way of life. Centuries of political turbulence and material peril drove men to seek peace in another world. Many of the rarer spirits saw no other path than that of saving the world by renouncing it. Prayer, poverty, and service, all voluntarily practised to the limits of endurance, must, they felt, bring out the best in themselves and in their surroundings alike. That was the monastic ideal in origin, dim though it so often became by growth of material power and privilege. Monastic music reflected monastic ideals.

Yet there were always men of equal fervour whose blood was too hot for contemplative inaction and discipline. Sometimes the Church absorbed them. They became fighting saints, against evil, disease,

94

and tyranny. This was most frequent when communities were young. As the monastic orders gradually acquired wealth and material influence they became themselves part of the accepted order of things, and they tolerated abuses and injustices which their founders would have fought to the last breath. The bolder minds were driven towards reform, and the natural inertia of a great institution often drove reform into revolt. Many a loyal son of the Church, guilty only of a burning desire to fulfil her original and express commands, found himself denounced as a heretic. The vast social upheaval which on its religious side is known as the Reformation, and on its cultural side as the Renaissance, was in essence a revolt of the layman against the inert and entrenched conservatism, spiritual, intellectual, or political, of a privileged hierarchy. The ferment was rising during just those centuries when the material resources of the Church were most lavishly displayed. At the time when her arts and her music were reaching heights never before approached, a new social and political philosophy was debating the whole foundation of her order. The ornate motets of Josquin were challenged by the congregational hymns of Luther.

Of the many influences which had a share in this general ferment two are especially noteworthy, both on intellectual and artistic grounds. One was the slow decay of Latin, the other the invention of printing. Dante is to us one of the great poets. We do not think of him as a scientist, or even as a theologian. But in his own day he was in fact using all the scientific and philosophical knowledge of his time as a background for his poetic genius. His opinions, and those of the Italian writers and poets who succeeded him, were opinions on what were then held to be matters of historical and scientific fact. These discussions were written in Italian, and Italian at once became a language of the first order. Great problems which had hitherto been examined almost exclusively in scholastic Latin were brought out into the daylight of a living speech. They became topics of wide and informed discussion among all classes of educated men, and among many more whose education was thus first stimulated. Religion and politics, art, music, and drama, all found themselves subject to vivid analysis and debate. Even in the field of classical literature itself, there appeared a formidable rival to Latin. Greek was rediscovered and brought with it the seething ideas and problems of the ancient Greek poets and philosophers. Greek scholars were brought to Italy and a fierce controversy arose in the universities of Europe as to whether Greek might or might not be admitted as a field of study comparable in a measure with the overwhelming claims of the Latinists. It is curious to reflect to-day that Greek was held, so comparatively recently, to be an unwarranted intruder in the academic groves.

In England Chaucer and Wycliffe were contemporaries, the one writing a panorama of English life and character which gave power and relish both to social thought and to vivid native speech, the other translating and interpreting the Bible in order that men might study it at first hand. In view of its enormous quantity, medieval art was very restricted in subject-matter. Lively and beautiful as it so often was, it yet touched only a small fraction of the sacred texts, and a very large number of what to us are the most important Biblical incidents and ideas were apparently quite unknown to the artists of the Middle Ages. The discovery and dissemination of the whole Bible was by far the most signal influence which moulded the intellectual character of the religious reformers. And this influence was inseparably connected with the use of living languages. Men might misunderstand the message. They could no longer ignore it.

Printing had already come when Luther's countrymen discovered the power of their own language and of the whole Bible almost simultaneously. Thereafter nothing could stop the march of knowledge and the communication of ideas, and in this fever of discussion and discovery the whole society of literate men and women could claim a share. In every sphere the spirit of exploration was triumphant. Columbus challenged the seas while Copernicus measured the heavens. Erasmus searched the minds and motives, while Luther purged the souls of men.

Nor were these searchings without marked effect on those who clung most tenaciously to the old order. The schisms and scandals of the Roman Church had been too notorious for her sincerest friends to gloss over. She had permitted the death of a Savonarola, and prosecuted with medieval fury a policy of repression, but she took steps to put her own house in some degree of order. Councils and decrees were frequent and drastic, and the most famous of these active inquiries, the Council of Trent, had artistic as well as ecclesiastical

96

ideals. The music of the Church had often tended towards an ornate and incongruous extravagance not unlike that which disfigured the lives of some of her prelates. The Council of Trent noted these things and resolved to adopt simpler and purer fashions of art. The music of Palestrina is an echo of these thoughts. It is by common consent the summit of sacred musicianship of the Roman allegiance. It is the last and finest fruit of five centuries of effort, purged of extravagance, perfect in taste and craftsmanship, sustained in nobility and serene emotion. It remains a model of all that was best in the cloistered church, but it was the last of its kind to win a universal tribute. Thereafter the development of the best church music passes in the main beyond the Alps. The future lay with Germany and its reformed Church.

Our own great Tudor school derived much of its character from Italy, but it had distinctive features of its own. There is in general a more bracing atmosphere, well suited to our climate and our speech. Our composers as a whole cared less for the impeccable smoothness of technique found in the best Italians. They are bolder and more angular, and not rarely deliberately harsh in the pursuit of original harmonies and in the illustration of verbal ideas. They were much nearer to the reformed text, and had their inspiration persisted they might well have achieved a synthesis between the past and the future. Their best works have a truth and directness of expression second to nothing in the whole range of music. But they were living on the edge of social and religious revolutions. They survived Palestrina by one generation and then their art perished in the conflicts of the sects.

German sacred music is founded on the Chorale, a broad congregational melody allied to a versified psalm or hymn. It is the insurgence of the nave in religious worship, and this in two ways. The nave will itself take part, but it will also listen intently for whatever message of inspiration or emphasis may be given by music to the literal text. The whole congregation sings its hymns, and the more specialized musicians, choir and organist, are expected to produce a music of their own, designed not solely for those who take an active part in it, but calculated also to make clear to the listeners the devotional or dramatic character of the chosen words. Protestant anthem and cantata are sung by the choir, but they are addressed to the nave. They must use a living language, and must try to interpret it adequately.

If a thousand people are to sing together, some form of musical discipline is essential. Melodies must move slowly and broadly, and there must be a frame of rhythm that will give the tune an appreciable pulse and form. In the matter of words too, the freedom of prose will not do. That is why the Psalms were put into metrical versions. The singing of Psalms in prose defeated, and still defeats, large congregations. The Anglican Church tries, by a free reciting-note followed by a bar or two of more formal melody, to make the best of both worlds, but only the highly trained can sing prose unanimously, and normal congregations must be content either to listen to the choir or follow it very tentatively. The Scots Psalter is a more consistent solution. The Psalms are ingeniously versified, and fitted to dignified congregational tunes. There are no difficulties of pace or metre, and the result is devotional music which every one can sing. The German Chorale uses exactly the same methods. The tunes themselves must be of suitable compass, and they must have no undue angularity either to pitch or rhythm. Above all, they must not attempt too much emotional or dramatic detail. The words are regular in metre and accent, but the verses vary in meaning. The tune has to fit them all impartially, and it should therefore express a general rather than a particular mood. Most of the unsatisfactory hymn-tunes are the fruit of a short-sighted desire to be moving or literal in the expression of detail. The tunes which have survived to be universally accepted in Protestant Europe are without exception dignified in style, smooth in melody, and steady in rhythm. They suit all kinds of voices, and every corporate mood of worship. They give us, perhaps for the first time in history, a truly democratic art.

The laymen not only brought their voices to the Church, they brought their instruments too. There is no doubt that the early Church was compelled to frown on instrumental music; if only by reason of its pagan associations. Moreover, from a purely musical point of view, most instruments were for long very crude in structure and could not begin to compete with the voice, either in quality of tone or range of expression. They were thus both secular in atmosphere and inferior in musical aptitude. Serious music, up to the time of the Reformation, is almost exclusively vocal. Reform brought all kinds of new influences, some transitory or incongruous, some permanent. In village and town where local musicians were to be found, their instruments began to appear and take a part in church music on festal or special occasions. This practice has survived almost to our own day, and there have been many conservative and isolated communities which contrived to withstand, for many generations, the almost universal adoption of the organ as the specifically religious instrument.

The organ can be traced back to quite early in the Middle Ages. We read of cumbrous mechanisms with many bellows, great levers for keys, and stentorian pipes. They seem to have been more astonishing than musical. In any case there was as yet no place for the organ as we know it. There was no music for it. So long as music was mainly one line of melody, it could never occur even to the most fertile inventor to do more than these early organs did; namely, reinforce one note at a time. Harmony had to come, before the possibility of a handy keyboard, suited to the playing of chords and simultaneous parts, could be thought of. With the development of harmony the keyboard rapidly assumed great importance, and the organ then began to find its way into every religious community which had the skill and wealth to construct one. The organist could there play all the parts in a complicated texture. The sustained tone of the instrument, together with its size and fitness for large spaces, made it the ideal medium for ceremonial effect. Its very lack of detailed expression made it admirably fitted to carry on the traditions of serenity and dignity so long associated with religious music. It soon became itself so rich in sacred memory and allusion that it was one of the most potent aids to the music of worship. That atmosphere it has permanently retained.

The first great organ school arose in Italy. Vocal harmonies were the framework of its music, but the Italians progressed with fine originality into the realm of a new and more instrumental style. They could take a plain-song as theme, and by means of the larger compass, the contrasted tones, and the flexibility of finger natural to the keyboard, could develop and embellish it far beyond the range of voices. This art they taught to their German pupils, who found in the reformed Church at home a wonderful field for the exercise of these powers. Nothing could be better suited to this artistic treatment than the Chorale-tunes which every one knew and loved. Nowhere is the essential grandeur, permanence, and fruitfulness of broadly conceived melody more manifest. There are thousands of these Chorale Preludes for the organ, of every type and mood. Some are worthy to rank with the greatest instrumental forms. Some, like the so-called 'Giant' Fugue of Bach, have reached world-wide familiarity. All are proof of the unique and abiding place which the Lutheran hymn had taken in Protestant music. From this time on, the sacred music of Germany is suffused with the warmth and nobility of these tunes. Their inflexions and cadences become the alphabet of her church musicians.

The music written for Protestant choirs used the various native translations of Bible, prayer-book, and hymns. The developing musical fashions of Opera and Oratorio, which we shall have to discuss later, were not slow to point the way to a musical treatment of the literal prose of the Bible. Simple settings of prose to a flexible succession of notes for a single voice might enhance the meaning of the words without altogether losing either the accents or the clarity of speech. In Passion music and Cantata it was possible to keep very close to the natural flow of prose by using this type of musical narration. Recitative, as it is called, is not difficult to follow if the words are already fairly familiar to the listener. The practice was in essence the same use of inflexion and cadence which had been imposed on liturgical Latin many centuries before. This musical Latin had remained fairly simple and intelligible so long as the Latin itself had kept its conventional pace and pronunciation, and it had in early times been tolerably well understood by those who sang it. But a living language is a far more powerful means of expression than a dead one, however venerable. Words in daily use cannot so easily be made into vocal exercises. They must always tend to retain a reasonable share of their natural shapes and values, and this is a healthy check on thoughtless emphasis and ornamentation. If in addition the words are taken from a text accounted literally sacred, the recited form should normally observe the rules of a simple artistic dignity. It was this plain telling of a story in music which held together the various elements in sacred music of narrative or descriptive type.

Two distinct uses of the chorus were also possible. It could personify the Apostles, or the soldiers, or the crowd of Jews, interjecting those words which were recorded as having been used

Dyson as a young man

North Parade Baptist Chapel,

HALIFAX.

•••••••••••••••••••••••••••••• ➤❧❦❧➤ ••••••••••••••••••••••••••••

AN

Organ Recital

WILL BE GIVEN BY

Mr. GEO, DYSON, F.R.C.O.,

(*Winner of a free Organ Scholarship at the Royal College of Music. London, Feb., 1900*)

On Tuesday Evening, April 3rd, 1900,

to commence at 7-45.

———◆———

Solo Violin - *Mr. J. NICHOLL BATES.*

ANTHEMS BY THE CHOIR.

ADMISSION FREE.

———

SILVER COLLECTION for Organ Renovation Fund.

Dyson included his own Sonata in C minor (no longer
extant) in this recital, given in 1900.

102

The first performance of *Quo Vadis*, Three Choirs Festival, Hereford, 1946; Dyson conducted.

TELEPHONE 8200.
AMBASSADOR 8200.

July 30th 1955.

Dear George Dyson

I think I must tell you about a dream I had a
few nights ago: I dreamt that I was at an orchestral
rehearsal and a symphony was being played. I came in
during the slow movement but did not pay much attention to
it: then came the scherzo which seemed extraordinarily
gracious and lovely - though I only remember one little
scrap of tune out of it

This does not look much in cold ink, but the effect when
I heard it was entrancing. I kept on wondering who it was by
then I saw Gerald Finzi, and asked him. And he told me it
was by you. Is there any hope that my dream will come
true ?

R Vaughan Williams

Letter to Dyson from Vaughan Williams, July 30 1955.

104

FROM SIR GEORGE DYSON

TELEPHONE :
WINCHESTER 4104   12.8.57   1 ST. JAMES' TERRACE,
WINCHESTER, HANTS.

My dear Herbert,

I'm very pleased and proud of this, and I'll practise my fingers on it in due course. I wonder if you have noticed that, in addition to the 'quote' at the end, there's my 'Pilgrims' first phrase in the left hand at the top of page 2. Don't mark it. It's anybody's figure, but it happens to come there, unconsciously, I expect. Good luck to the whole piece, and thank you.

Our love to you both

Yours ever

George D.

Letter from Dyson to Herbert Howells in 1957, thanking him for the Dyson movement in *Howells' Clavichord.*

105

At the Hereford Three Choirs Festival in 1936 (left to right): Dr Herbert Sumsion, Sir George Dyson, Sir Percy Hull and Sir Ivor Atkins.

23 July 49

Dear Friend

Thank you for sending me your symphony which I am going to study as soon as the present pressure of work is less.

I have been wanting to write to you for a long time, but tours and other work have crowded my time.

I enjoyed so much conducting your CANTERBURY PILGRIMS OVERTURE, and the audience and the orchestra were most (enthused.) I think it is a masterpiece of characterization. The kind of lusty energy and humour that Chaucer portrayed you have expressed in the medium of music to perfection. I was so happy to conduct this remarkable music with memories of the time when we were students together.

Next time I visit England, I hope you will have a little leisure so that we can spend some time together talking of the old days and of the days to come.

Your friend

Copas

Hound Hill Road
North Greenwich
Connecticut

A `Yankee word meaning enthusiastic !`)

Letter from
Leopold Stokowski
to Dyson in 1949
following a performance
Stokowski had given of
the *Canterbury
Pilgrims* overture.

Above: Dyson with
his son, Freeman, and
grandson (c.1955).

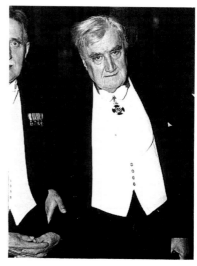

Right: Dyson (left) with
Vaughan Williams after dinner
in 1952. (Lady Dyson bisected
her husband in order to fit the
photo into a frame she already
possessed).

by a number of people. This was an obvious dramatic effect of great power. And the chorus could also be used to represent the whole body of Christian worshippers. It could sing a devotional or contemplative number which expressed the feelings of the general congregation of believers at any suitable moment in the unfolding of the story. This practice was in very close touch with the past, and it helped to transfer to the Protestant churches some of that atmosphere of reflective devotion which was characteristic of the best monastic music. It was that same art of the choir, select in skill and sympathy, yet turned more definitely, by the use of a living language, towards the expectant and understanding ear of the whole body of the Church.

All these features of a new and more congregational form of worship found their most fruitful soil in Germany, where an intense fervour of reform was allied to native seriousness of character and to a musical sensitiveness of remarkable depth and extent. Many generations of her organists, now mostly forgotten, devoted themselves to providing music of this reformed and congregational yet eminently sacred character. They played their Chorales, they accompanied the congregation, and they used their more trained singers and players to provide musical settings of Psalms and sacred stories, devised so as to throw into relief the chief incidents, but never losing touch with the essentially corporate aim of the whole method. For it must never be forgotten that the German Passions and Cantatas were in the strictest sense religious services. They were not sacred concerts. Hymns and Psalms, prayers and sermons, musical narrative and reflection, were all parts of a general and congregational order of worship, in which every person present had an active and appropriate share to fulfil. This brought the congregation, the organ, the choir and such orchestral instruments as were at hand, into an intimate and religious community of purpose such as had never before been achieved. We are beginning to appreciate the unique and lasting character of this music by our growing attention to the Passions and Cantatas of Bach. At a distance of two hundred years his work stands out above all his predecessors and contemporaries, but he was one only of a very large number of men working to these ideals. The summit of their beauty is found in Bach, but he was, no less than Palestrina, the culminating point of a long tradition. He was the glorious end of two centuries of effort.

Bach learnt his organ-playing from men whose predecessors had inherited what was best in the pioneer school of Italy. He applied it as they did to his beloved Chorales and to great detached pieces of analogous style. He provided for his choir and orchestra music of the prevailing religious type. There is in him a supreme combination of all that a thousand years of church music had developed, but he invented hardly at all. He found a method of sacred composition and used it consummately. The details of his Protestant environment were already fixed. These he applied, in reflective choruses, in sacred narrative, in dramatic contrast, and in the adornment of congregational hymns. We perform his Cantatas to-day, sometimes in a church, sometimes in a concert-hall. In both places they are, to us, sacred concerts. They were not concerts to Bach. They were to him what High Mass was to Palestrina. Instead of the priestly offices of the Mass, the Lutheran cantata had its preacher and his sermon. Instead of the catholic congregation passively receptive of a priestly blessing, there was an active body of worshippers, listening to suitable homilies and singing its own praises in its own tongue. The Mass is in perpetual danger, now as in the Middle Ages, of becoming by elaboration more and more remote from the universal expression of a general devotion. That could not so easily happen to Bach's services, because the congregation was an integral and controlling part of them. Organ, orchestra, choir, and soloists might display a specialized art, but at every pause in the narrative the whole congregation with corporate voice gave the occasion its living and present acceptance. Its hymns were the background against which the more highly organized music was projected. The thoughts thus expressed in its own language determined the character of the whole service, both as a profession of faith and as the practice of an art. Bach's music comes neither from the cloister nor from the study. It is a layman's worship, written with the fervour of an evangel, and with the skill of genius.

Those branches of the Church which remained true to the Roman allegiance did not escape the democratic infection, but their response to it took a different and less consistent form. The laity were not actively incorporated in the services, after the German fashion, but a very definite appeal was made to their artistic sense. Sacerdotal tradition was too strong to permit an integral co-operation of all the members of the Church in its use and government, but the Church began to import from outside the musical resources which were so rapidly accumulating in other spheres. Palestrina was the end of the old era. After his death all the more active spirits turned to the theatre, and the rising tide of Opera was by far the most potent musical influence in seventeenth-century Italy. When the Church wished to add to its own more traditional resources, the appeal of the new dramatic music was irresistible. This new music had its own problems, but for the moment we are concerned with the reactions in the Church. The temptation to use the new dramatic technique in all music, whether sacred or secular, could not be withstood, and when the Church set out to enlarge its musical horizon, it found itself borrowing wholesale from the theatre. Composers, players, and singers were brought over from their daily occupation with the stage, and encouraged to give the Church a taste of those new methods of musical expression which practice in the theatre had taught them.

It is clear that many of the most sensitive composers were uncomfortable under this system. They frequently show a most curious diversity of styles. They seem to have felt that the operatic method was not really convincing in the old sacred surroundings. Writing, as they often did, for voices only, they retained much of the purity and serenity of atmosphere which belonged to the older order. When, however, they were commissioned to employ the whole musical apparatus of the theatre, soloists, chorus, and orchestra, they found it impossible to resist those technical devices which the stage had suggested. The same composer would write church music in one style for one occasion, and church music of a totally different type for another. And there was unfortunately no doubt which the congregation liked best. Prelates and people both demanded just those kinds of musical effect which they heard and applauded in the theatre. The result was that the older church music, so truly consonant with the deepest religious aspirations, began to appear outworn, while its place was taken by what in secular surroundings was a form of dramatic entertainment. And a dramatic entertainment it remained, whether within the Church or outside it.

To St. Jerome, in ancient days, is attributed the saying that 'a Christian maiden ought not even to know what a flute is'. This sentiment must be interpreted in the light of those Pagan festivals of instrumental music which were often accompanied by less admirable features which the early Church so passionately opposed. Zealous saints were acutely conscious that a custom perfectly innocent in itself may by evil association bring very undesirable practices in its train. That was why St. Jerome, in common with many later saints, drew what appears to be so arbitrary a line between flutes and voices. Could he have watched the fashions of Italian church music in the seventeenth and eighteenth centuries, he would have felt the wisdom of his attitude to be only too abundantly proved. Apart from the growing use of the organ, there was no such thing as sacred instrumental music. The Italian orchestra was formed and trained in the theatre, and it could not suddenly become something else when it walked over to the Church. The famous solo singers equally belonged to the stage. There they had learnt the arts of public performance. They could not change their methods by stepping from a secular to a sacred platform. Composers might be given sacred words to set, but these words were Latin, often but dimly or crudely understood, and the natural attitude to words of every kind became that which was daily adopted in the theatre. To composers, as to their patrons, there was every temptation to use that type of music which was so warmly acclaimed by the public support of opera. Given the means of the theatre, they adopted the theatrical style, and the record of their work is a record of the progressive degeneration of elaborate sacred offices until they became little more than a fashionable entertainment. Appeal to a thoughtless public taste had met with its invariable fate. It reached the lowest common standard of value.

The contrast between the church music of Italy and that of Germany, during the hundred and fifty years which separated Bach from Palestrina, is extraordinarily vivid. There is not, on the surface, such a very great difference of means. The Germans developed a strong feeling for dramatic representation of ideas in music, and they employed soloists, chorus, and orchestra. But these things grew up within the Church itself, and that Church had both the strength of its reforming piety and the impregnable rock of its translated Bible. It was also a democratic Church, not only in public appeal, but in actual foundation. The Church in Italy was popular enough. People flocked to hear its elaborate concerts. But the German congregation was very much more than an audience. It had passed through fire and sword to reach a conscious ideal of religious faith and freedom. That ideal touched the humblest as well as the greatest of its sons. The music of Bach was its artistic embodiment. Elsewhere the quality of church music was clearly in decline long before Bach was born. It is a still further tribute to him and to his countrymen that they pursued their own high aims with such continued integrity.

The decline was not confined to Italy. Our English diarist Evelyn could write in 1663:

> One of His Majesty's chaplains preached; after which, instead of the ancient, grave, and solemn wind music accompanying the organ, was introduced a concert of twenty-four violins between every pause, after the French fantastical light way, better suiting to a tavern, or playhouse, than a church.

France, Austria, and Catholic Germany caught the contagion, and during the course of the eighteenth century the fashionable Masses written and used in the most august surroundings were often of a shallowness and incongruity beyond belief. The dance-tunes, the orchestral ritornelli, the vocal flourishes, the pseudo-dramatic choruses, all were frankly transported from the theatre to the church; and every serious contemporary witness has testified to a growing degradation of taste. So popular was the importation, so influentially supported, that Europe has hardly yet recovered from it, and of its baneful consequences there is at least one overwhelming proof. Since the operatic movement arose in Italy in the seventeenth century, no liturgical work of supreme quality has been written within that Church. Bach's Mass in B minor was not written for liturgical use, nor has it been so used. Beethoven's Mass in D is a sacred symphony, also written outside the Church. Mozart's Requiem Mass has the poignancy of his last days, but what is the repute of all the conventional Masses which he and the two Haydns and Schubert wrote? They are less convincing works of their respective composers. Genius itself could do nothing with the style of church music prevailing in their day.

Reformers, and there have been many, have long been thoroughly alive to these facts. Facile melody, conventional choruses and glib orchestration do not make church music, even at the hands of great talent. Reform in every country finds itself returning to the sixteenth century, to the schools of Palestrina and the Tudors, when what is felt to be the truest idiom of the old Catholic worship last found expression.

Nor are the Protestant churches in much better case. Since Bach died in 1750, no great master has found work for his whole talent within the Protestant communion. A few truly devotional works, like the German Requiem of Brahms, were written outside it. So were all the great sacred epics of the concert-room. The Church borrows from these masterpieces. She no longer creates them. And there are only two possible explanations of this artistic dearth. Either no musician of supreme endowment has found himself in the service of the Church, a chance so improbable that it may be dismissed, or else the Church has consistently failed to offer a sensitive ear and an adequate scope for his genius. Bach's gifts died with him. Not for a century after his death did they win external tribute. Like Palestrina, he had no true successors, and the new fashions of musical display buried his work for generations. One clear example of this blindness to real artistic and devotional values may be seen in quite recent times, and very near home.

When, towards the end of the nineteenth century, an influential section of the Anglican Church began to advocate and develop a more ornate liturgical ceremonial, it was not to Palestrina, or Byrd, or Bach, that they turned for appropriate music. They imported Masses of the later Italian order, sometimes further sentimentalized by passage through France, and they offered these showy productions as the principal musical ornaments of an English Choral Communion. We need not wonder at the naiveties of a village church cantata. Such crude and theatrical ideas were not invented in the remote countryside. Their models were sung and endorsed by fashionable metropolitan churches, by people who claimed to be in the van of ecclesiastical and artistic progress. They did not lack sincerity. What they lacked was knowledge. Religious music, like religious ritual, should come spontaneously from within, and it should express, not a temporary or superficial appeal to the ear, but a devotion of the whole mind, as deep and as disciplined as the ancient liturgy itself.

Such, in broadest outline, has been the place of music as handmaid to the Church. Our English cathedral can teach us much about these varied ideals of the past, for her unbroken historical continuity has kept traces of them all. That continuity has also saved her from being the exclusive servant of any temporary fashion, however powerful. Her versicles and responses, her chanted canticles and psalms, are echoes of the Middle Ages. Her congregational hymns are products of the Reformation and of some subsequent revivals. There are hymns translated from early or medieval Latin. There are hymns from the rediscovered Greek. A large number come from Germany and from the Scots Psalter. Many have been culled from the poets, or written to express ethical ideals. Her tunes are equally varied. A few belong in spirit to the plain-song of the Middle Ages. Many more, and these of the best, are German Chorales or Scots psalm-tunes. There is also a fine group of specifically English tunes, mostly from the eighteenth century, which are as dignified as the German, yet show the definitely native love of a strong rolling rhythm. The Methodist revival of the early nineteenth century stimulated a much needed revival in the Anglican Church itself. The hymns of the Wesleys came into the Church, and so, unfortunately, did many later revivalist tunes. Missionary fervour was held to excuse excess of sentiment and crude musicianship. Some of the popular hymn-tunes of the nineteenth century were the musical equivalent of a too fervid oratory. They illustrate the historical fact that all the worst religious music has been written by two classes of writer. The one is without any genuinely religious emotion whatever. The other has nothing else. The abysmal Masses of the eighteenth century were written by musicians of poor religious taste. Much of the music of our nineteenth century was written by evangelists sadly deficient in musical taste.

The Anglican anthem is our equivalent for the Latin motet of Rome on the one hand, and the German cantata on the other. The Latin motets were of the polyphonic school, using the perfect vocal technique of the liturgy to adorn select passages of the Latin Bible and prayer-book. Our great Tudor anthems apply this same method to the English text. It survives in Tallis, Byrd, Gibbons, and their contemporaries, whose music now claims a growing favour; and it is frequently imitated, with a wider harmonic horizon, by modern writers. We have never adopted the German cantata as a whole, but the narrative and descriptive features of it are found in a large proportion of our anthems. Purcell is the first great representative of the post-Reformation style which for so long supplanted the old

115

liturgical music almost completely. He, like the Italians, worked largely in the theatre, but his taste was saved from the most serious lapses by two causes. His genius was too original and too fertile to follow a commonplace convention rigidly, and he was held, both by education and by the conditions of his work, very close to the sacred text. No composer ever had a finer sense of the value of words. His words were of the English Bible, and not even a Restoration court could ignore their inspired grandeur. To the people as a whole they were of clear and divine portent, and Purcell at his best was worthy of them. His free use of soloists is in tune with the new fashions of his time. So are his frequent orchestral interludes. We rarely hear his church music as he wrote it, but it has many permanent beauties.

Thereafter English church music fell into a backwater, and who shall say, in view of what happened elsewhere, that this was not a partial blessing? We lacked the German intensity, but we were spared the Italian shallowness. Many generations of competent organists continued to write services and anthems of undistinguished, but at the same time of solid and useful, quality. A few, like the Wesleys, had flashes of real genius. Sebastian Wesley is probably a clear case of a man who, had he enjoyed the opportunities given to some of the great men abroad, would have made masterpieces of European repute. His gifts would have filled a much broader sphere, had the English Church of his time possessed the means fitly to employ him. The less talented men, though rarely inspired, never lost a fair sense of religious fitness, and to them also the majestic English of the services was a constant education and safeguard. Moreover, in spite of revolution and dissent, both within and without, the English Church retained, and still retains, much of the internal organization of the Middle Ages. Canons, clergy, and choir still sit in the same order, and often in the same carved stalls, which their monastic predecessors occupied. Our choir still consists of lay clerks and boys.

It often surprises our Protestant kinsmen abroad that we have clung so tenaciously to this narrow view of the type of voice appropriate to the Church. Our men altos in particular seem to some of our visitors strange and unnatural. But the Anglican choir is a monastic survival, and with it have survived these traditions of monastic music. The passionless tone of boys' voices suits the passionless serenity of contemplative worship. Our altos are trained to produce the nearest equivalent to that smooth and restful tone. Mellowed by the echoes of a great building, it is in spirit the oldest music we know. The Anglican choir is not a choral society. It is a special and delicate instrument for the production of special and delicate effects, and it has fifteen hundred years of proved experience behind it. We have seen what happened to those churches which imported the prima-donna and the operatic chorus instead. We have no reason to envy them. Our cathedral organist, with his men and boys, may have made no great mark in the world, but he and they have preserved an atmosphere, bequeathed from the long past, which carries with it an ideal of religious and musical intimacy not easily to be matched in our less restful age. The Anglican anthem, written for this special choir, may be but a modest contribution to the story of music, but it is often a very fragrant one.

As for the organ itself, we owe to it more than we are wont to realize. For the mass of men, and for many generations, it was the most serious instrumental music they could know. It was the training-ground of innumerable musicians, both here and abroad, and the significance of its influence is shown by the fact that so many of our chief institutional appointments have for centuries been the accepted preserve of the organist. Cathedrals, universities, and schools have all made the organ-loft the centre of their musical life, and many of them, but for the organ, might never have admitted music at all, on anything approaching its present integral status. This custom too is monastic in origin and goes very deeply into our sense of fitness. When a new college or school builds a chapel and installs an organ, it is obeying an instinct which has its roots in the monastic schools of the Middle Ages, and this tradition is stronger in England than anywhere else because the initial concentration of religion, education, and art under the same endowments has never been completely broken. Classical organ-music owes much of its character to this long association. Ordered worship and educated taste have spared it much meretricious handling. 'Orchestral' organ-playing is a modern notion, more ingenious than convincing. Mechanism can now offer a play-box of queer stops and restless combinations which are often thoroughly retrograde. They may serve an ephemeral purpose in other places, but they do not belong to the art of classical organ-playing, as generations of fine organists have taught it. The organ was evolved for broad effects. It also demands impeccable clarity of taste. Then, and only then, is it in tune with its noblest traditions.

The history of English church music is not an inglorious one. It had a fair share in the Tudor masterpieces, and that was only the summit of what had been a very long period of discovery and achievement. If, since then, it has created little, it has preserved much. It still gives us what, as part of the whole church of Western Christendom in the Middle Ages, it helped to create, a glimpse of the abiding foundations of our music. As we pursue the further story of the art we shall have to admit that most of the later masterpieces have been evolved elsewhere, and the question arises as to whether the essentially creative spirit of music will ever return again to its earlier haunts; to those great cathedrals, for example, near one of which we have spent this discursive hour? Must Cantata and Oratorio be consigned, more often than not, to the concert-hall, while the great churches and cathedrals pursue their more exclusive path? A few have opened their doors, but these wonderful buildings, which by magnificence and tradition should house all the masterpieces of every art, are too often empty and silent. Some of her own music the Church retains. Her walls are periodically filled by the corporate devotions of her own people. But will she ever again become the mother of all endeavour, the home of all sorts and conditions of artists, of all professions and denominations, bringing the best they can do? Will the great orchestral symphonies ever find a natural home in the wide spaces of her nave? Will the ethereal beauty of a string quartet secure a corner in one of her transepts? These are questions to which the Church herself can alone find answer.[1]

(from *The Progress of Music*)

---

1. Recent years have seen Dyson's wish fulfilled in a way he would never have anticipated; i.e. in the widespread tendency to use London churches and chapels for recording purposes (on account of their superb acoustics). Dyson's own *Hierusalem* was recorded in St Mary's Church, Westbourne Green, in November 1983; his *Three Rhapsodies* for string quartet in Rosslyn Hill Chapel, Hampstead, in December 1984; his *Tabard Inn Overture*, *In Honour of the City* and *Sweet Thames run softly* in All Saint's, Tooting, in April 1985; and his *Christmas Garland* in St Jude's Church, Hampstead, in March 1986 (all London locations). A generous selection of Dyson's church and organ music was recorded in Jesus College and St Catharine's College, Cambridge, in the summer of 1986, and his *Prelude Fantasy and Chaconne* for cello and piano in St James', Clesherwell, in September 1987.

Of Organs and Organists (i)

There is a group of distinguished organists which occasionally meets round the same table. They have been called 'A Choir of Great Swells'. And not without reason, for there is no more able and versatile branch of the musical profession. The place of the organist in musical history is remarkable. Tallis and Weelkes, John Blow and Purcell, Bach and Handel, to take typical names at random, and scores of their contemporaries in each characteristic period and place, belong to the succession. The English roll is both eminent and unbroken down to our own day. And it is remarkably comprehensive. I once jokingly suggested a series of monographs on famous organists, to begin with Sir Arthur Sullivan, Sir Henry Wood, and Dr. Vaughan Williams, all of whom held important church appointments in London. Also in or near the organ-loft were Mackenzie, Parry and Stanford, John Ireland, Herbert Howells and Malcolm Sargent. I have purposely omitted the names of men known only or mainly as organists. It is the extraordinary range of ability, of which organ-playing is a part, which I want to demonstrate. And if we were to include choristers also, there is a whole additional array of outstanding names, from Palestrina to William Walton.

Some time ago an important administrative musical appointment was made, and an independent observer quite truly and justly remarked: 'Of course, another organist'. Organists do in fact tend to occupy a very large proportion of the institutional and administrative posts in our musical world, and the origin of this preponderance goes far back into our musical history. For many centuries there were virtually only two ways in which a serious musician could contrive to earn his bread. He had to serve either a church or a court. The Church had wide affiliations with universities, colleges and collegiate schools. A court might be that of a prince, a noble, or a civic institution which could maintain the more pronouncedly secular arts. Every musician of note, up to the end of the eighteenth century, was attached either to a branch of the Church or to some secular source of patronage. This was true of continental Europe as a whole, and true of England too, though in a more restricted sense. Court patronage of the continental type never became permanent in England. We have had no actively musical royal house since the Tudors, and when the patronage of the

Court is tenuous and intermittent, the lower ranks of the nobility have no model or fashion to follow. In England, therefore, the Court has taken a smaller share, and the Church a larger, in the employment of musicians, than was customary on the Continent. We have had nothing parallel to the high secular patronage of Italy, France and Germany.

It was the medieval church which created the vocal polyphony on which our western music is founded, and the organ was a mechanical imitation of that technique. It is the only instrument on which a single pair of hands can maintain sustained harmonies. Concerted instrumental music, however, was predominantly secular in origin. It arose partly in the pageantry of kings and cities, and partly through the domestic practice of 'voices and viols'. The wind instruments of military or municipal ceremonial joined the stringed instruments of more intimate entertainment, and together they became the orchestra as we know it. This orchestra accompanied the birth of oratorio and opera and then began to extend its overtures and interludes into concertos and symphonies. In this very rough-and-ready generalization of musical history England has played no distinctive part since the days of 'voices and viols'. We have borrowed continental fashions from time to time, but only during the last hundred years have we joined and contributed to the main stream of European music.

For at least three centuries, therefore, our one unbroken tradition has been that of the Church, its Bible and Prayer Book, its versicles, psalms, hymns, canticles, and anthems. The descriptive anthem is oratorio in miniature, and that is why oratorio appeals to us so directly. It embodies the two deepest channels of our musical history. It is choral, and it is Biblical. Parallel with these traditions came the gradual acceptance of the organ as incomparably the most suitable instrument for ecclesiastical use; and as there was virtually no alternative home for musicians of appropriate talent, they became organists, choirmasters and church composers. Had there been in England the princely or civic patronage of the courts and cities of the continent, our players and composers would have had a wider choice and a greater secular security. One can feel the latent dramatic and symphonic urge of men like Greene, Battishill, Boyce and the Wesleys, but they had to write in the main for the resources at their command, the cathedral choir and organ. Arne, who was outside the Church, never found permanent security for his great talents.

These organists and their successors have done two things. They have fostered a style of playing suited to churches rather than to concert-halls, and they have maintained the vocal purity of the cathedral choir and its music. Our monster organs of today, with their facile wealth of mechanical registration, culminating in the fantastic boxes of tricks to which so many listeners become inured in the cinema, have debased both the style of many players and the taste of many hearers. The essential quality of an organ lies in the 'voicing' of its single stops. If these are uneven or unsympathetic, then fancy combinations may be no more than devices for hiding the inherent poverty of the sound. The austere beauty of the single pipes, and the family of pipes 'voiced' to merge into one another: this is the proper basis of the organ and its technique. A few stops perfectly voiced have, in their own field, an aristocratic quality analogous to that of the string quartet among instruments in concert. If the beauty of an even and passionless tone does not appeal to us, then the organ is not our favourite. Much of the prevailing search for odd colours and combinations is due to impatience with organ tone as such. The dynamic fireworks and the incessant vibrato of the orchestra have blunted our taste. The organ is more exacting. It demands a more ascetic, absorbent and contemplative attitude.

A similar discipline governs the cathedral choir. Its essence is the boy's voice. Its men are at their best when they blend with that clean white tone. There are infinite gradations of volume and quality within the accepted range, but a cathedral choir destroys itself if it attempts to compete with the secular mixed chorus. And its most characteristic music has the same canons of fitness. It moves comparatively slowly because it must play on the arches of the building. Its background is reflection rather than action. It accords with a sensitive ear and a mind at ease. The handling of such music and of its more modest parallel in church and chapel has been the early stimulus and training ground of countless musicians.

In addition to these musical factors, the organist inevitably learns something of the personal and administrative problems of an institution. He must both teach and learn, rule and be ruled. Further, he is usually the musical centre of a circle much wider than his church. The organist of a parish church may be the conductor of a choral and orchestral society, a lecturer and adjudicator over a wide area, a performer and teacher of distinction, and even a competent composer of music suited to his experience or resources. There is no position in the profession more varied and more influential in range.

Add to the cathedrals and churches the universities, the colleges, and the more musical schools, and we have by far the most widespread and permanent spheres of musical endeavour in Britain. These have been our musical nurseries for centuries, and many of our most gifted men have spent their whole lives in them. Others have plunged into the secular world as performers, conductors, composers or administrators, after their formative years in or near the organ loft. That is why the organist is so ubiquitous in our musical life. There was no other institutional ladder for the aspiring youngster, and the system fed itself. The pupil was attracted to the master and strove to emulate him and follow his career.

There is one further historical fact which distinguishes the normal environment of the organ and which should give the organist a poise and a perspective. If a man would live again the musical history of a thousand years, let him sit in the choir of a cathedral and listen. There he will hear the monotone and inflections of primitive chanting, the perfected melodic art of plainsong, the fundamental diatonic harmonies, the gradual elaboration and ultimate maturity of vocal polyphony, the contemplative motet or canticle or the descriptive anthem, the whole being varied, contrasted or supported by the wealth and range of the organ and diffused by the echoing spaces of nave and transepts. There are today many more lively introductions to music. But is there anything more genuinely fundamental, more balanced in mood, more perfect in style, more sensitive and disciplined in emotion, more steadfast in musical faith? I doubt it.

(*The Musical Times*, November 1952)

Of Organs and Organists (ii)

One of the habits of increasing age is to talk more and more about the past, and one of the trials of the younger folk is having to listen to these wandering reminiscences. But I am going to indulge myself today by recalling events long gone, and you, I hope, will not be made too impatient by hearing of them.

It is fifty-seven years ago this July that I first invaded the portals of the Royal College of Organists, then housed in Hart Street, Bloomsbury. I was fourteen, and still dressed in short trousers and what was then called a 'sailor' blouse, with an open front and a square collar hanging down behind. I wanted to be an A.R.C.O. and had the cheek to try. By a fortunate indulgence of the examiners I passed the playing tests, but no indulgence could then swallow my paper work, and it was not until eighteen months later that I became a proud Associate. After a further year I became a Fellow at sixteen, in January 1900. But I was not a record-breaker. Sir William Harris, as he now is, had become a Fellow a year before me, while he was still only fifteen. I have never forgiven him.

The organ on which I played and practised in a little chapel up in Yorkshire had two manuals, and the tracker action was so heavy that to play on the Great with the Swell coupled needed some very hard finger-digging. The pedal board was flat and square and stopped at E, so that when I had to prepare, as an examination piece, that Sonata movement by Alan Gray which opens with a pedal solo high C followed by high F, I had to kick the side-frame for my F. I enjoyed giving it a firm dig at the examination. My organ was of course blown by hand, at a tariff of fourpence an hour, and the sturdy friend who blew for me seemed to think he was helping in a good cause.

I have sometimes thought that the Royal College of Organists might well have dedicated some kind of memorial to the stalwart and devoted organ-blowers of those days. Many of them were great characters. Some of us on this platform still remember with affection a past caretaker of the Royal College of Music, Bernard Parker, who pumped the wind into every kind of organ music for so many years that he was an infallible critic of even the most accomplished playing. You could not get a wrong note or a smudged entry past him. He knew the notes as well as Sir Walter Parratt himself; and he made no secret of his opinion of any flashy or incompetent player who monkeyed with the text. We should salute with honour the memory of him and his like.

Heavy and clumsy as it was by today's standards, there was something to be said for the old tracker action. You felt that you were in direct touch with the pipes, as a wind-instrument player is when he fingers his keys. Albert Schweitzer has written about this. Your phrasing was under more exact control than it is with a pneumatic or electric action, where you may not be quite certain at what point in the lowering or raising of a key the actual sound begins or ends. The modern mechanism comes between you and the palettes. Registration, too, was a very different problem before we invented these rows of composition pistons that a loose thumb can twiddle about with, whether you look at the stops or not. We had a few combination pedals, but effective registration had to be, in the main, the direct handling of the stop-knobs. And the knobs themselves had their whims and humours. There are still a good many large continental organs with stop-knobs of sturdy size which draw about six inches, if you have the time and strength to pull them. It is often advisable, I am told, to have two assistants, one on each side, who can take a firm grip, put one foot against the case, and get a real purchase on the stops. Registration under the old conditions was an exercise as well as an art, and the managing of the stops had a direct effect on your style. You did not make fussy and unnecessary changes, and you had to choose both your stops and the moment of handling them with great care. You learnt to sympathize with old Bach, who so often wrote 'Full Organ' at the beginning of a piece. With the kind of mechanism he had to master, it was no doubt best to take your coat off, pull out everything in sight, and then blaze away.

The recital players whose names were most familiar in my boyhood days up north were W. T. Best of Liverpool, who was succeeded by Dr. A. L. Pearce, and Kendrick Pyne at Manchester. Best published numerous arrangements and editions of his repertory, all highly skilled but not always particularly faithful to the original sources. Dr. Pearce wrote a Sonata da Camera which looked classical enough and played easily enough to be everybody's meat. And there was a very popular player from Rochdale, David Clegg, who had his own collapsible organ which he packed in vans and travelled about with, erecting it in various halls and playing on it with marvellous dexterity. One of his special treats was the representation of a thunder-storm, and he was not the only organist in those days who gave us thunder and lightning on demand. In London E. H. Lemare was the rising young virtuoso star, creating new standards of manipulative skill by his Wagner transcriptions. He had one blind spot, however. He refused to select me as his assistant, a decision which possibly helped his career, and no doubt modified mine.

The music some of us played in those days was a very mixed bag indeed. The programme of my first full-scale concert recital, in 1900, included Mendelssohn's sixth sonata and Bach's Toccata, Adagio and Fugue in C major, but it also contained a long group of what we then considered to be the more modern spicy bits, by Guilmant, Lefébure-Wély, Alfred Hollins the blind organist, Lemare, and a march by William Faulkes, of which I now remember nothing whatever. One of my own show-pieces at that time was my own arrangement of the *Tannhäuser* overture. The organist's world was then full of arrangements of all kinds, and it is both easy and natural to smile at those ingenuities now, whether they were good or bad in themselves. But we must remember that in a provincial town there was then little or no chance of hearing orchestral music at first hand. I first heard Wagner on a brass band, and the organ was the obvious instrument for imitating, as best one could, the tonal variety of an orchestra. These organ transcriptions belonged to the same category as Liszt's elaborate transcriptions for the piano, and there was a whole library of overtures and symphonies arranged for piano duet which were a staple fare of good domestic music.

During my student days in London I was organist of Greenwich Parish Church, where Thomas Tallis was said to have played nearly four centuries ago. I cannot say that it was his organ I played on, but it was certainly of a venerable age. For it had a very old three-manual tracker action and the keyboards were a curiosity. The white keys were black, and the black keys had a white inlaid strip, such as you find in some old spinets. These manuals are now fittingly preserved in a glass case in the church.

One last reminiscence of those days. At a Sunday afternoon concert in the Albert Hall in 1901, I played with my teacher, Dr. W.S. Hoyte, the Merkel Duet Sonata for the organ. We sat on the stool side by side, and as Dr. Hoyte was roughly three times as broad as me, it must have been a moving sight. How we found our respective pedals or shared the stops, I cannot now imagine, but I have a recollection of one of my thin hands being often involved with one of his fat ones. It is a pity the cinema reel with its sound-track did not then exist to record our performance. And what a scoop it would have been for television!

And now I must try to be serious. The most potent and beneficial influence on the technique and taste of organ-playing during the period of which I am speaking was unquestionably that of Sir Walter Parratt, who both by his own example, and by the standards he demanded from his pupils, set a model of which we enjoy the fruits today. The list of his pupils, and of the younger men they have trained in their turn, is a very distinguished one indeed. Nor must we forget the whole succession of cathedral organists, from Wesley down to our own time, who upheld the more restrained and dignified atmosphere proper to their special field of activity.

But it is the work that organists have done outside the organ-loft which is perhaps the most remarkable feature of British music in the history of the last hundred years or more. Sullivan, Mackenzie, Stanford and Parry were all at one period of their lives in or near the organ loft. Henry J. Wood began his career as an organist. And of men now living, Vaughan Williams is a Fellow of this College and played in a London church, William Walton was a chorister, Malcolm Sargent both chorister and organist, to name only three. In addition to the specialized music which organists and choirs have created and maintained in churches and cathedrals, they have been the guardians and nurseries of musical talents of all kinds, and these sources have provided a very large proportion of the skill and enthusiasm which has culminated in the proud position Britain holds in the musical world of today. No organist need hide his head. He belongs to a long line of gifted and devoted men who have served and adorned not only their own traditions, but the broader world outside as well.

This is my last address as your President, and I should like my last words to be of gratitude for the past, encouragement of the present, and faith in the future. May the highest achievements and ideals of our profession be long maintained, and may our organists long continue to stimulate all that is best in the social and artistic life of our whole musical commonwealth.

(RCO President's Address, July 1954; printed in *The Musical Times*, October 1954)

Of Organs and Organists (iii)

When I first began to think about the subject of my talk to you to-day, 'The place of the Organist in British musical life', it naturally reminded me of the fact that I myself began to play regular services on

Sundays at the age of 13, and during many later years I played daily services and gave more organ recitals than I can remember. If, therefore, our organists have any special place in the story of British music, I can perhaps share a small personal corner in it. It is also inevitable that in looking back over my own 60 years of musical life, I shall be tempted to speak of events and experiences that came directly under my own observation. It has been said with truth that 'reminiscences are among the sharpest weapons in the armoury of old age'. And it is equally true that one of the trials of younger folk is having to listen to them. I apologise therefore at once for the personal memories I may recall, and I hope you will not find them either too tedious, or too narrow in their range.

I came to London and became an organ student at the Royal College of Music in the year 1900. At that time, as before and since, one of the most perfect examples of music in Christian worship was to be found in the Temple Church. I hope none of our over-seas visitors will fail to visit that historic and unique building which, after being so badly damaged by war, has now been worthily restored by the generous body of lawyers whose special heritage it is. At the time of which I am speaking, the organist of the Temple Church was Dr. (later Sir) Walford Davies, whose name became a household word through his inimitable broadcasts about music, devised to interest and inform the ordinary listener. Dr. Davies was also a Professor at the Royal College, and in one of his small classes were four organ students. He invited us to attend his full choir practices at the Temple on Saturday afternoons, and after the practice we played and extemporised at each other on the organ, under the inspiring guidance and friendship of Dr. Davies himself. These were unforgettable occasions, and I want to tell you what happened to those four young men. One, alas, died young and could not fulfil his promise. The other three are still active, but in most diverse ways. Of this trio, one was William Harris, now Sir William Harris, organist of St. George's Chapel, Windsor, and known to us all as a consummate organist and choir-trainer, a distinguished composer of sacred music, the musical head of those many Royal services and ceremonies uniquely associated with Windsor Castle, and everybody's friend in our Anglican musical world. Harris followed what I will call the straight path of an exceptionally gifted organist – a parish church, a cathedral, New College and Christ

127

Church at Oxford, and finally Windsor, where he is now. He has been faithful to the organ-loft, but that has not prevented him from conducting choral societies, teaching at the Royal College, and above all exercising a powerful influence for good, both in university musical circles, and in our Royal School of Church Music.

The second member of our trio will certainly interest, and may surprise, some of our over-seas guests. He was Leopold Stokowski. He became organist of St. James's, Piccadilly, went thence to New York and later to Philadelphia. There he developed and displayed a genius for orchestral training and conducting all the more astonishing in that it was, in his student days, totally unsuspected. He made his Philadelphia Orchestra, by common consent, the finest modern orchestra in the world, and none of us will ever forget the impact of his gramophone records when they first reached us in Europe. He became, and has remained, one of the supreme leaders and interpreters in that most exacting of all musical professions. And those of us who knew him more than 50 years ago may be forgiven if we feel the romance of that lad, for he was hardly more, then a modest young organist, becoming a world celebrity, with a record of orchestral achievement unsurpassed in our time.[1]

Is this the kind of eminence to which a young organist might aspire? For Stokowski is not unique. Two of the most skilled and versatile orchestral conductors we have ever had in Britain, the late Sir Henry Wood, and Sir Malcolm Sargent now, were both reared in the organ-loft. Indeed Sir Malcolm has often said that the foundations of his

---

1. Over 40 years later, Stokowski wrote a marvellous letter to Dyson à propos the *Tabard Inn* Overture. It is reproduced on p. 000. Since writing the sleeve-note for the Unicorn-Kanchana recording of this work I have come across Dyson's own programme-note, which reads as follows:-
This overture is a frank and light-hearted 'curtain-raiser' to *The Canterbury Pilgrims*. All the themes are taken from the main work and introduce, as it were, the chief characters in Chaucer's Prologue. Their tunes appear roughly in this order: the Franklin at his supper, with some slighter allusions to the Monk and the Nun; a quiet section from The Poor Parson; the Doctor's lively Apothecary followed by the robust Merchant, the rolling Shipman, and a hint at the Sergeant of the Law; another flowing and quicker tune from the Epilogue with a following crescendo; finally the Wife of Bath and a general jollification. The Overture is scored for a normal full orchestra, and is intended to be followed immediately by the soft semi-chorus with which the main work begins:- 'When that April with his showers sweet ...

musicianship were laid when he was a chorister and organist under that exacting teacher Dr. Keeton, at Peterborough Cathedral. Dr. Keeton was one of those old-fashioned tyrants who made his assistants memorise their music and play fluently from a figured bass. He would not tolerate any modern 'arrangement' of an old score.

And now, if I may, something of myself, the third survivor of our little group. I have become neither a leader in church circles nor a distinguished organist, like Harris, nor have I carried out a totally different career like Stokowski. My field, for better or worse, has been musical education, and my experience is not uncommon among organists of my time. Few young men can guess what is in store for them. We three, in those far-off days, looked for a busy church or, if we were fortunate, perhaps a cathedral, as our goal. But only Harris remained true to form, and achieved this. My own fate, when I was looking for work, was to be sent as organist and music-master to a school, and I directed the music of one school after another, until finally I found myself head of the Royal College of Music itself.

Most of my life has been spent in what in England we call 'public' schools. And I must explain to our visitors that we call them 'public' because they are essentially 'private'. I know of no other more logical reason. They are not a part of our statutory educational system. They are boarding schools for boys, founded, endowed and maintained by private benefactions and substantial fees. There are a number of such schools in other English-speaking lands, but they are a specifically English product, with a history of many centuries.

I should like to talk to you about one of them, Winchester College, because I was organist and master of music there for many years, and in some quite fundamental respects, Winchester is an original model of them all. It was founded in 1392, a hundred years before Columbus reached America. It was built by that great Bishop and Chancellor, equally powerful and famous both as priest and administrator, William of Wykeham; and it was part of a twin foundation, the other half being New College at Oxford. Fifty years later Eton College at Windsor and King's College at Cambridge followed the same pattern, Eton's first headmaster and some of his staff being imported from Winchester.

Now it is impossible to understand the plan of Winchester College unless we realise that it was from the first a strictly vocational school.

It was as strictly vocational as a modern technical college. A modern college of science, for instance, exists to produce scientists. Winchester College was designed to produce priests. The boys were to pass from Winchester to Oxford, to proceed to University degrees and Holy Orders, and to become the priests and administrators of church and state, of the type of that supreme example, William of Wykeham himself.

The terrible plague of the fourteenth century, known as 'the black death', had decimated the countryside, including the priesthood of that period. William wanted to recruit and train young priests, and the statutes and curriculum of Winchester were designed to that end. The language was Latin, then universal in church, law-court, and every learned context. But as the bias of Winchester was above all religious, it must have a worthy building, a College Chapel of great architectural beauty and distinction, the inspired model of many later Chapels elsewhere, and the centre of its corporate life. Further, these young boys were to be in daily contact with the liturgy of the Church, and there must therefore be, in addition to governors and teachers, a group of chaplains to say the services and a choir to sing them. The College was built to house 70 scholars and 16 Quiristers, and although the number of resident pupils has grown in modern times from 70 to 500, the 16 Quiristers are still there, and when I was appointed to direct the music of that Chapel, I became the lineal descendant of that priest who first trained and supervised those choristers nearly 600 years ago. Among my predecessors were Thomas Weelkes, the madrigal composer of the early 17th century, James Kent, whose 18th-century church music is still alive, and Samuel Sebastian Wesley, the famous organist and composer of the 19th century. What I want to stress is that this foundation of a collegiate choir at Winchester is one of those precise points at which music became an integral part of our educational tradition. The pattern of Eton was similar, and the many famous boarding schools which have since been founded have, almost without exception, followed tradition to this extent, that they have made the school or college chapel the accepted centre and symbol of their ideals. They may not have a collegiate choir in name, but they have a skilled organist, and they make up a daily choir of boys and staff who can sing canticles and anthems of cathedral standard. They too have adopted this musical legacy of the medieval monastic school.

I must not gossip too much about Winchester, but history there is very real. There is still a tradition that the best cook the College has had was a French prisoner-of-war captured at Agincourt in 1415. When our present Queen Elizabeth II visited the College she could be welcomed with the same ceremony that greeted Elizabeth I in 1574. And it is said that a comparatively recent Librarian complained of the difficulty of keeping the Library in perfect order, because many of its treasures, he protested, had already been moved twice since the Reformation!

The period of the Reformation brings us to a second crucial event in this educational story. The dissolution of the monasteries brought to an end the monastic schools as such, though many of them survived or were refounded as secular Grammar schools for day-boys. Winchester and Eton were spared owing to their close connection with the universities. Of strictly musical and ecclesiastical foundation we were left with the cathedral choirs, the collegiate chapels of Oxford and Cambridge, the royal chapels like Westminster Abbey and St. George's Windsor, and the two schools of Eton and Winchester.

The Reformation in England was a highly complicated and fluctuating movement, and it ended in a compromise. We denied the authority of Rome, but we did not entirely abolish the Roman Liturgy. We translated it into English, suppressing or modifying some of its doctrines in the process. We forbade the use of Latin, and inflicted severe penalties for any infraction of these reforms.

But we left a loop-hole for Latin in the Universities, and in 'our two schools of Eton and Winchester'; they might still sing Latin without penalty.

In other countries the Protestant Reformation took a far more drastic course. It abolished the monastic structure and forbade the Roman Liturgy entirely. In England we could and did adapt the old Latin church music to English words. Some of our 16th-century composers openly wrote for both languages. There was no real break in the musical tradition. But in Scotland and northern Europe there was for a long time a profound gulf between past and present. Germany gradually evolved its Passion music and sacred cantatas, but in many Protestant communities sacred music, apart from congregational hymns and metrical psalms, virtually died. In France, Italy and Spain the old music continued, but this was in Latin. Only in

England could the people hear sacred music of high rank sung to them, year in and year out, in their own mother tongue.

I believe this singing of services in English to be the real foundation of our exceptionally strong choral tradition. Even the Nonconformist bodies ultimately formed their own mixed choirs, and these choirs began to sing anthems and choruses derived from the established Church. This music and these singers were the nucleus of the innumerable choral societies which grew up in the industrial revolution of the 19th century, when concentrated populations began, quite spontaneously, to organise their own local musical events. Glees, part-songs and secular cantatas were added to their repertory, and the final result was a frequency and range of choral performances unparalleled anywhere else in the world. I remember, not many years ago, a distinguished foreign conductor telling me with obvious pride that he was going back home to conduct a rare performance of the B minor Mass. I forebore to tell him that in England we sing it, on an average, about once a week.

And now I want to say something about the effect of these developments on the organist himself. First a further word about schools and colleges. With the growth of amateur music in the outside world came a demand for more varied and secular music inside the schools. It was not difficult to organise a choral society, but boys wanted to play as well as to sing, and as there was already a professional musician at the organ, he must come out of his organ-loft and teach them. The organist thus became a music-master as well, and as he was rarely an instrumentalist, apart from at the piano, he must have assistants to teach the aspiring violinists or cellists, and perhaps also a retired band-master to supervise the playing of wind instruments. The pioneer example of this expansion took place at Uppingham School, where that great headmaster, Dr. Thring, deliberately set out to build a complete orchestra inside the school's own walls. He imported gifted teachers, he invited famous artists to give recitals and create a taste and an enthusiastic desire for the best music, and he did in fact create by far the best school orchestra then existing. The example of Uppingham was quickly emulated by other boarding schools whose size and resources permitted a similar musical policy, and in a comparatively short time there was a substantial group of such schools, which made orchestral music an integral part of their leisure activities.

132

They played and sang many quite major works. Some of them built a special music school. All had a musical staff; and the organist became, willy-nilly, a director of music, head of a department, and approximate in rank to his classical, mathematical, or scientific colleagues. That was my position at Winchester, and the change from that to the Royal College of Music was a change from amateur to professional standards, but not a change of taste or ideals ...

Outside the strictly educational field, the sphere of the parish church and cathedral organist has immensely widened. Most of our permanent choral and orchestral societies have been formed under the leadership of a local organist. He, too, has emerged from his organ-loft and accepted broader responsibilities. Our most outstanding case of this trend was and is the annual festival of the Three Choirs of Gloucester, Hereford and Worcester, which has produced as many classics and as many new works of large proportions as any comparable organisation in the world. These three organists are expected to be of high competence, not only in the domain of cathedral music, but also in the larger world of the choral and orchestral repertory they have to select, rehearse and conduct ...

Organists have no need for pessimism. It is a good life. A familiar organ to play, and the fine traditions of five centuries of church music to uphold; a local choral or orchestral society to conduct; recitals on his own organ and an occasional engagement to play elsewhere; a group of private pupils, both practical and theoretical; lectures under an educational authorities' programme; musical work in a school, a technical institute or a training college; arranging or scoring music for strings and organ, for a performance or a service in the church; perhaps an organ-piece or an anthem to compose; these things are all supremely worth doing, and provide both a stimulus and a satisfaction which does not fade ...

(Part of the RCO Lecture, delivered before the International Congress of Organists in the Senate House, University of London, 31 July 1958)

The Artist and Society

... If the holocaust of our century was a sudden, blind, and inexplicable suicide of European civilization, for which no rational cause can be discerned, then the idea of social progress is a myth, and we are all struggling victims of a tragic fate. But if there were in fact predisposing strains and symptoms that we can analyse and define, then we must expose them without gloss or reservation. It is both misleading and dishonest to identify an apparently cultured order with what we find good in it, ignoring or disguising the evils which are equally a part of that social fabric. If we extol, for example, the artistic and scientific achievements of the nineteenth century, we must equally admit that either these or some other irresistibly powerful factors produced the ruthless destruction of the twentieth.

This issue was put to me most forcibly by a German refugee teacher towards the end of the Second World War. He had escaped from the Hitler machine some years before and was working as an education officer among German prisoners of war in England. I had asked him to tell me frankly what, in his opinion, had contributed most to the political deterioration, the virtual self-destruction, of the most highly organized, the most technically efficient, and by tradition one of the most intellectually and artistically gifted nations in the world. His answer was startling, for he expressed it in the one word: Education. He held it to be precisely the unparalleled success and efficiency of the German educational system which had led inevitably to the national tragedy. And he added that we in England were not safe from the same danger.

His argument was this: that the very processes of mass education, practised in the integrated industrial communities of our time, could and did produce the soil in which these monstrous weeds of hysteria and hate could suddenly appear and grow beyond control. We made our people literate without teaching them to think. We gave them technical skills without any controlling judgement. We stimulated their ardour and energy without any commensurate ethical or emotional discipline. We thus made them into the easy victims of any plausible political theory, and at the same time ensured that they would be diabolically effective agents of aims and purposes of which they might see neither the direction nor the end. Given but one great nation with this ruthless power, then every other nation must either bow to it or create a comparable strength with which to fight it. One country can make a war. It takes at least two to maintain even a local peace.

It was characteristic of his German origin that my acquaintance had an intense interest in literature and the arts. But he pointed out how marked had been the morbid and destructive elements in some of the art and writing of the late nineteenth and early twentieth centuries; the denial or ridicule of tried ideals; the refusal to accept even the most basic conventions; the prying fascination and analysis of abnormality; the recurrent themes of distortion, cruelty, and self-pity; all these were applied to the exploitation of callow or unthinking audiences. Such were the symptoms of a fundamental social malaise which education had signally failed either to control or cure. And the devices of propaganda, based on the twin pivots of narrow literacy and rigid regimentation, had immeasurably increased the risk and intensity of ungovernable waves of misunderstanding and prejudice. Thus had Europe been swept into the abyss, Germany being at once the chief offender and the chief political victim.

Unless and until, he argued, we realize that among our deeper instincts there are some so potentially evil and destructive that they must at all costs be controlled, the urge and energy they engender being guided into more creative and beneficial channels, there can be no hope of a secure future for civilized humanity. If our social and educational systems cannot achieve this, and no one can deny that in the perspective of recent history their effects have been lamentably inadequate, then they must either be changed or we shall destroy ourselves in the very effort of self-preservation.

The social problem has two aspects. There is an increasing lack of personal and creative opportunity in the mechanical process of industry, to which so large a proportion of our population is tied. Yet these very processes provide a greater margin of leisure which should be filled by active and beneficial pursuits. If our education makes us into no more than technically efficient workers, it leaves the growing surplus of our time and energy ignored and frustrated, and we become the prey of unrest and faction. Men make war in their spare time. In the middle ages, when the sowing and garnering of crops, the tending of cattle, and the essential handicrafts of life demanded the full day's labour of a whole community through most of the year, there was certainly less time and fewer resources for fighting. Armies were small and seasonal. It was impossible to harness a whole nation for conflict, for neither armaments nor food could be produced and squandered at will. Nor was there anything equivalent to our modern apparatus for disseminating news, opinion, and propaganda. Heads had more time to think and longer to cool, while the hard toil of bare existence could neither be neglected nor relegated to machines.

Today we have enough surplus industrial power and such facilities for the accumulation of material that we can permanently conscript armies and factories for what we call defence and our neighbours call war. We can mobilize virtually the whole nation either for good or evil. Our newspapers and broadcasts can arouse an aggressive fervour almost overnight, and we have twice in this century seen the world plunged into a life-and-death struggle for survival which every man who had time to think and was not politically insane knew could result only in the ruin of victors and vanquished alike. Who can deny that we can devote our spare energies and the margin of our free hours and days to building up reserves of power, and that we can use mass-education and propaganda to inflame public opinion to bursting point? We have virtually no choice, for a modern political machine can easily fall into a few autocratic hands, and we are involved before we know it in a blind struggle we can neither avoid nor localize.

We are all familiar with the dilemma of the scientist. He provides us with a constant stream of inventions and a growing command of resources which can be used either to good or to evil ends. What is he to do? Should he turn politician? Should he hide or suppress his discoveries? Should we dragoon or suppress him? We have found no rational solution of this problem. Science itself has no frontiers, and the scientist would prefer to devote his genius and skill openly and without reserve to mankind as a whole. But this means that any unscrupulous individual or community can capture his products and use them for selfish or destructive purposes. And every competitor is then impelled to a like defence.

And what of the artist? Is he to go on fiddling while Rome burns? Why does he fiddle at all? Is he to seek for an ivory tower in the hope that he will escape the world's turmoil? Or is he to play to anyone who will listen, in the hope and faith that his art may help at least to relieve the distraction of his fellow-men?

My German acquaintance may have been too acutely depressed by his own personal history and environment. He may have over-simplified his statement of the educational problem. But if by education we mean the whole process of preparing ourselves for social and civilized life, and if, when we reach what should be mature citizenship, we have no reliable command either of our own passions or those of our rulers, then the failure is patent and tragic. Either we are incorrigible or we do not know how to educate ourselves.

There are three types of men who have consistently fought the apparent chaos of the world. They are the saints, the prophets, and the artists. The saints have preserved, sometimes in loneliness, sometimes through the ministry of a chosen few, more rarely by a successful appeal to the civic virtues of a community, a faith in those spiritual and ethical values which are the basis of all religions and of all genuine human betterment. The prophets include all who passionately pursue the truth and fearlessly proclaim it. Theirs is the creed of the enquirer, the scientist, the sage, and the philosopher. The artist distils from his imagination an intuition of order and proportion, on which he builds a sensitive and convincing interpretation of the world of appearances and emotions. These are the three faiths, in the latent good, the honest knowledge, and the creative arts of mankind, which poets, priests, and evangelists have extolled since man first learnt to define and express his thoughts. They are, or should be, the goal of all education, of which textbooks and methods are but the technical shadows. Human sympathy, objective truth, and disciplined taste are the ideals which all our devices of selection and nurture should serve.

The artist has two tasks. He must express his own sense of values, his exceptional awareness of the pageant of nature, his interpretation of human environment, his crystallized emotion in face of appearances and events. But he has also the social function of evoking a comparable response in those to whom his art is addressed. We are all potential artists in so far as we can follow the thoughts and

137

share the intuitions of poets or painters or musicians. But we are also much more than this, in that we can all put some measure of creative order and energy into the tasks or recreations of our own lives. And if, as is now so often the case, we have to earn our bread in the monotonous or mechanical routine of an office or factory, it is all the more imperative that our leisure should be devoted to more personal and satisfying ends. Books should give us knowledge, sympathy and a touch of wisdom, drama a more vivid consciousness of human and social problems, the fine arts a window through which we see the graces and ornaments of life. Music should carry us into a world of imagery and sensitiveness of sound which at its lowest is a respite and at its highest a revelation and a renewal. 'The man that hath no music in his soul is fit for treasons, stratagems and spoils. Let no such man be trusted.' Broaden this definition to include the harmonies of all the arts and we are not far from the ideal of all education of the spirit.

I once heard an old teacher say: 'Whatever is worth doing at all, is worth doing badly.' By which he meant that the sheer pleasure or discipline of making and doing is in itself a major good, however clumsy the hand and however faulty the product. We who are artists by profession should retain a measure of humility in presence of the amateur, for it is by him we live. It is he who spares us the toil of providing for our material wants, who sets us apart to create, and who gives us whatever rewards our arts may earn. And if he is himself something of a creator too, so much deeper and more permanent will be his support of our craft.

Every child is both appreciative and creative. The degree to which these instincts are lost or overlaid in the passage of years, through adolescence to adult life, is a measure of our failure to provide an outlet for those marginal interests which should grow into the enlightened pursuits of leisure hours. It is the idle mind which is the prey of slogans, of tendentious facts, of prejudiced and self-centred emotion. It is the passive spectator who is most susceptible to fickle and superficial fashions. If we could make the arts a conscious and integral part of our whole social structure, we should have achieved at least a potent contribution to the sanity and permanence of our civilization. We should have provided a balance, a sense of proportion, a release and freedom, both mental and spiritual, which might well mitigate the strains and anxieties of political and national strife. We might even persuade men that the fellowship of the arts, which transcends all the barriers of race and language, is a not too fanciful model of what human relations might become in other spheres.

These considerations should appeal especially to the musician, for his is essentially a social art. Men and women of most diverse types, and of every degree of gift, can not only listen but can take a part in the making of music, though their contribution may be no more than one voice among hundreds. My own experience covers the whole hierarchy of music-makers, from the solitary and detached composer spinning his imaginary web of sound, to the massed festival of a thousand performers. It is some of the facets of this enormous mass of endeavour that I shall attempt to describe. It is their value as an artistic and corporate activity which is my main excuse for being a musician at all. If I may paraphrase a sentence Dr. Johnson used in another context: A man is rarely more innocently employed than when he is making music.

(from *Fiddling while Rome Burns*)

Music and the Ordinary Listener

... Like all professional musicians, I am often asked by my friends to explain something in music which puzzles or bewilders them. They say to me: 'I can't understand it. Can you help me?' This happens more especially with regard to new music. Now the weakness of most so-called explanations of the arts is that they don't explain. Indeed it often seems that the more you try to explain the further away you get from what you are asked to describe.

It is rather like trying to explain a sunset. Science may tell you that the dust in the air causes a differential diffraction of the various wave-lengths of light, but that could hardly help anyone to imagine the beauty of what he has seen, or describe it to anyone else. A waterfall could, I suppose, be described as a combination of oxygen and hydrogen wearing a channel in geological strata, but that would give no-one any notion of what Niagara is like. John Ruskin, that great exponent of the arts, used to give an example of this inherent difficulty of explaining what we see. He asked: 'What makes grass green?' and was told it was due to a substance called chlorophyll. Then he said:

139

'And what is chlorophyll?' and was told: 'It is the green matter in plants'. And there you are.

Ask me to explain a Fugue, for example, and I can tell you it has a theme called the subject, and another called the answer, and the parts come in one at a time with the same subject, and there are various changes of key, imitations, episodes and so forth. But none of these words can tell you anything about the music itself, and even they are only a kind of diagram, which often fits a dull fugue better than an inspired one, because inspiration may pay little attention to strict rules. In the same way, if you ask me to tell you about a Sonata, I can say there are contrasted themes and keys, modulations, developments, repetitions, codas, and so on; but the more words I use, the further away I get from the actual music I am supposed to be discussing. The fact is that one cannot put music into words at all, and such descriptions have no musical meaning unless you are first of all familiar with the music itself and can bear it in mind.

What then should the listener do? In my opinion, nothing, as a first stage. Let the music flow over you. If from time to time it evokes in you a feeling of sympathetic response, that is the beginning of musical appreciation. This may eventually grow into a warm familiarity with a whole language of musical thoughts. Only then can verbal descriptions or comparisons begin to make sense. And there may be a great deal of music which never grips you at all. I know hundreds of works which satisfy me profoundly. I know many that leave me cold, and some that definitely repel me. These last are not, for me, what I seek in music, whatever anyone else may feel or say about them. Let us first be open-minded, and then perfectly honest about our tried reactions and tastes. That is the only way to a genuine appreciation of any of the arts. We can of course gossip about the lives of composers and about the circumstances under which they wrote. But our only real musical experience is that of the music itself, and there is no substitute for it.

(from *Introduction to Celebrity Recital*,
Kyla Greenbaum, 28 June 1955)

Tempo Ordinario

I have been concerned in these talks mainly about Time in music, and I want to mention tonight a curiously interesting time-measure which I came across a day or two ago, a measure often used by Handel and his contemporaries in the 18th century – 'tempo ordinario', 'ordinary time'. Now what did Handel mean by it? I am sure he was thinking of ordinary singers and players, the ordinary competent musicians of his time, and *he* was sure that they would all know what ordinary time was. It is a refreshing reminder of that common humanity and common experience that may belong to us all – composer, player and listener alike. There is perhaps for all of us a continuity of average musical pace and thought which Handel described as 'ordinary time', and of course it is also evidence of Handel's own wide humanity – no frills, no introspection, no attempting to bully us or surprise us or puzzle us, just ordinary music at an ordinary pace for ordinary singers and ordinary listeners. 'Tempo ordinario' surely refers to the sort of straightforward piece that people of normal susceptibilities, or normal response, can perform and listen to with pleasure ... For we are never to forget that time in music is not a mechanism. It is not a matter of soulless mechanical beats. Musical time is like the pulse of life; it has alternation of stresses and releases; it is part of our own living experience, not a machine-made apparatus coming from outside. And, if we don't live our music, feeling and comprehending it as part of our own experience, then it means no more to us than the ticking of a clock.

There are really no ordinary listeners in any uniform sense. Every listener is an individual – a unique personality with unique experience and unique responses to music as to everything else; and I venture to use the word 'biological' to express that essentially living and personal aspect of time in music. And our biological times may differ profoundly. Why should I expect my mind, for instance, to keep pace with that of an exceptionally great and gifted man? I can only follow him haltingly at first, gradually understanding what he has to unfold, and only very gradually reaching the essential inspiration that may have come to him in a flash. That is why all great art has to be lived with before we can get the best out of it; and then, try as we may, we differ enormously in our capacity for understanding. Some of us are slow, some of us do not respond easily, many of us only respond to music of very simple and straightforward types; very few of us are sympathetic to all kinds of music.

Let us admit all this quite frankly, and not seek to disguise or minimise it. The first requisite in artistic experience is complete honesty; but though we may honestly agree that we differ in our appreciation, there are yet some things we nearly all have in common. One of the most fundamental of these is our response to the various rhythmic patterns which are the background of most of our music. These give us a prevailing mood − a sense of urgency, perhaps, or of rest, of speed, or of passion or of contemplation − and in these indications of mood, just as in the simple pulses of time, there is a fundamental bias towards two phases: stress followed by release. These I refer to what I believe to be the prime cause − the two-phase rhythms of life itself as we know it, whether it be the beat of the heart, the march of your feet, day and night, winter and summer, life and death. *Recurrent* rhythms are essentially primitive in nature; people whose main interest is simply the beating out of recurrent rhythms are either very young musically, or else their taste has been spoilt. I have no doubt at all about that. Rhythm, if you like, is fundamental, but it is really the *beginning* − it is the background, not the end, of music. The most deep and tender things go far beyond mere rhythms − they go into spiritual realms of contemplation, of rhapsody, where time is perhaps no more than the dim reminder of the passing of all things.

Now all great men know how to wait: they realise the supreme importance not only of what you say, but of when you say it. Young and immature minds are impatient; they have no sense of proportion; they fling ideas at you unprepared, undigested. Far more artistic works fail by confusion of ideas than by lack of them. If I insisted on putting something striking into every bar I played to you, then you will very soon cease to pay any real attention at all. A picture that is all highlights is unbearable; an orator who emphasises everything he says leaves us irritated or bored rather than enlightened. It is like the old Gilbertian line: 'When everybody's somebody then no-one's anybody'. You must have light and shadow − in Art as in everything else ...

... The great man knows how to wait, how to prepare, how to please us, how to make us expectant, how to give us his best thought just when we are likely to be most ready to receive it. Let me give you one or two examples. The Brahms Violin Concerto begins with six bars of the chord of D major. When it does change — to ordinary dominant harmony — the change is refreshing because we have been made to wait; then after *that* bar comes a marvellous change of harmony into a comparatively remote key, which is effective simply because the background — the home key of D — is there:

The most marvellous example of all is the beginning of Wagner's *Ring* which is a series of four immense operas. First is the *Rheingold*, the beginning of which is 136 bars of the chords of E flat. It begins with long-held notes without any movement at all, then a slow arpeggio, then arpeggios which get more and more ornate; but the chord itself never changes. The bass holds an E flat for 136 bars. It takes between three and four minutes to play. Now the fact that Wagner could dare to do it — that he could believe that anybody could sit for that length of time listening to one chord — is a measure of the size of his mind. That chord — that two or three minutes of the chord of E flat — is the beginning of a long music drama of four operas which is going to involve, say 15 or 16 solid hours of music. It is impossible to have too firm a foundation for a work of that length and complexity; Wagner felt that he was going to make a very long speech indeed and that it must be well prepared. And when the shift to a new chord finally does take place, it has the effect it does because Wagner could wait ... (from *Music and the Ordinary Listener*, BBC Third Programme, 19 May 1937)

Time and Tone

... So far as sheer command of an instrument is concerned, many young performers today compare with the most accomplished artists of the past. What they have still to acquire is experience and maturity of style, and this prompts the questions: 'What do we mean by style? What holds our delighted attention when we hear a convincing performer?'

Many years ago, in Berlin, I heard three famous violinists play the Beethoven Violin Concerto on three successive nights. It was a most stimulating experience, for they all differed in a hundred details, yet all three were quite convincing. In this problem of interpretation I am quite sure that one most vital element is what I would call timing. If it were possible to play a piece of music in absolutely strict mechanical time, we should soon want it to stop. If it were possible to play with absolutely unvaried tone we should cease to listen. These two elements, variations of tone controlled by variations of time, bring the music to life, and it is the combination of these subtleties, both in detail and in the whole architecture of a long movement, which creates what we feel to be the artist's personal style.

There is an interesting parallel in the graphic arts. A photograph may be absolutely accurate, yet quite lifeless, while a drawing of the same face, though not so mechanically exact in its lines, may yet be a far more vivid likeness. The artist in fact selects and emphasises certain features which seem to him, and to us, especially characteristic of his sitter. He must not overdo these features, or the result is a caricature, but it is precisely in these subtle distortions and exaggerations that his artistry consists. And, like my three violinists, three different artists might produce three different versions of the same subject, yet each one of them could be a living and satisfying portrait.

When a composer puts notes on paper, and says we are to play or sing them at a certain speed, he does not mean an unvarying mechanical pace. When he marks a passage soft or loud, he does not mean that every note is to be equally soft or loud. He expects, and so do we who listen, that the player or singer will apply a personal and distinctive interpretation of the printed signs, and this interpretation is in fact an endless succession of subtle variations of time and tone. It is these which give interest and vitality to the music. Yet the performer must not exaggerate them to the point of restlessness. He has to find that happy mean which is at the same time faithful to the composer, to himself, and to the expectation and response of the listener. This convincing command of expression distinguishes his style and rank as an artist ...

(from *Introduction to Celebrity Recital*, Moiseiwitsch, 24 May 1955)

Architecture and Proportion

Recently I spoke of those slight but constant flexibilities of time and tone which make the detailed phrases and rhythms of music expressive and alive. They are too subtle to be written, but music would be very dull without them. Now I want to say something of this interpretative power on a larger scale, and I cannot do better than begin with a story about that great pianist of the nineteenth century, Anton Rubinstein. He was a man of superb gifts, both technical and musical, but he sometimes showed his mastery in ways that were both wilful and unorthodox.

One of those personal interpretations was his playing of the well-known Funeral March in Chopin's Sonata in B flat minor. He would begin with a touch so soft as to be barely audible, and then slowly pile up a crescendo so gradual that at any particular moment you were hardly conscious of it, but which continued inevitably and relentlessly right up to the middle of the middle section, which Chopin had in fact marked quite differently. Having arrived at the utmost fortissimo of which the piano was capable, Rubinstein would then equally slowly and relentlessly contrive a long and almost imperceptible diminuendo which at the end of the march just vanished into silence. A distinguished musician who heard him wrote of this performance: 'The way Rubinstein can control his tone is not merely difficult; it is impossible!'

That was an extreme example of an artist's interpretative power applied to the whole range of a long movement, and this faculty of unwavering and extended control, this ability to think in long periods, restraining oneself in order the better to bring out the most significant features or climaxes of a whole work, is one of the sure signs of genius, both in the composer and in his interpreter. Think of the long cumulative fugues and massive choruses of Bach. Think of the hundred climaxes in Beethoven; how skilfully they are prepared, controlled and placed in the grand architecture of a movement.

This sense of timing on a large scale is what we mean when we speak of symphonic development and grandeur: the feeling that a whole composition has an aesthetic purport in which details have their significant place, but are not allowed to interrupt the unfolding of a massive and powerful design. I have always felt that one of the most remarkable examples of timing in this sense is the beginning of Wagner's *Ring. Das Rheingold* consists of the slow building-up of a single chord for over 100 bars. Such a beginning would be ridiculous in a small work. For *The Ring* it sets a time-scale, a monumental opening for a monumental work. All the greater composers, and all the finest performers, have had this instinctive sense of proportion, this power of saying big things in a big way ...

(from *Introduction to Celebrity Recital*, Campoli, 21 June 1955)

Music and Words

... The combination of words and music is a fascinating study, and I should like to say something about the way in which composers have approached the problem of fitting music to a poem. In the case of the old ballads and folk-songs, there may be no attempt to illustrate the actual words at all. So long as the melody is singable and given the right emphasis to the metre of the poem, that is all that is necessary, and the same tune fits all the piece. And there have been poets, like Robert Burns, who wrote new poems to fit old tunes. The old accompaniments, if any, were as simple as possible, just a few chords, or a harp-like musical figure, such as a wandering minstrel might have played as he sang.

But later composers have rarely been satisfied with so simple a method. They wanted to add something to a poem by allowing their musical imagination to create an accompaniment that would enhance or illustrate the vocal setting of the words, and there are broadly two ways of doing this. The composer may look at the poem as a whole and provide a musical background which is of one chosen and prevailing mood throughout. Schubert's *Erl-King* is an example of this method. The poem tells a most dramatic story, with many changes of speed and emotion, but Schubert prefers to think mainly of horse and rider galloping through the storm, and this headlong fever of the accompaniment never stops. Similarly in *The Trout* he invents a darting figure which suggests the quick movements of the fish itself, and this is the musical background of the whole poem.

The other method of dealing with words is more fluid and dramatic. It looks at what the poem is saying from verse to verse, or even from line to line, and it tries to vary the mood of the music in keeping with the moving incidents or emotions of the words. Schubert's *The Wanderer* is a simple example of this method. Some sections of this song illustrate the sorrows of the pilgrim, some depict his more joyful recollections. It is the method of music and drama on the stage, where you find every degree of intimacy between what the singer is saying and the music that clothes it. The danger of the method is that the music may become scrappy and inconsequent. The test of mastery is the composer's ability to provide apt and convincing illustrations of detail, without losing control of the design and proportions of the work as a whole ...

(from *Introduction to Celebrity Recital*, Elisabeth Schwarzkopf,
BBC World Service, 14 June 1955)

The Amateur Professional

For centuries there was often no great gulf between the amateur and the professional, and musical history is full of noble, and even of royal patrons, who were themselves practical musicians as well as generous supporters of music. Let me give you an example, taken from a memoir of nearly four hundred years ago. The year is 1564, and the writer is Sir John Nelvil, who was sent by Mary, Queen of Scots, as her ambassador to our Queen Elizabeth. He writes:

'After dinner my Lord Hunsdean drew me up to a quiet gallery that I might hear the Queen Elizabeth play upon the Virginals. After I had hearkened a while, I moved the tapestry that hung before the door of the chamber, and seeing her back was toward the door, I entered and stood a pretty space hearing her play excellently well. But she left off immediately, so soon as she turned and saw me, and came forward, seeming to strike me with her hand, alleging that she used not to play before men, but when she was solitary, to shun melancholy. She enquired whether my Queen or she played best, and I found myself obliged to give her the praise.'

That last feminine touch brings the great Elizabeth to life more than a page of formal history. No wonder the court of the Tudor period attracted its galaxies of talent. And one might compile a long list of such enlightened princes and nobles in the following centuries. Perhaps the most famous of all was King Frederick the Great of Prussia with his flute. Everyone knows the story of Bach's visit to him, when Bach played to the King, and the King played to Bach ... (from *Introduction to Celebrity Recital*, Bronislav Gimpel, BBC World Service, 31 May 1955)

Teaching Today

One far-reaching consequence of recording and broadcasting has been a remarkable improvement in the aims and methods of teaching. Gifted children are born where Providence wills. Most of the world's great artists have come from comparatively small and obscure towns and villages, and they had to learn and be taught as best they could.

Imagine the position of a provincial teacher fifty years ago; a rare concert, perhaps, in his own or a neighbouring town, nothing else to feed on but his own past experience and the music he could make for himself. I know this well; for when I came to London from Yorkshire at the age of sixteen, I had heard very little beyond the local music of my home town.

Today the teacher can be in daily and immediate touch with a wealth of fine performances of every kind, and this affects his whole attitude to the task of training and guiding the gifted child. In particular, I think we have now got rid of most of those narrow methods of teaching which were mechanical exercises rather than music. Whenever I hear the word 'method' used in this narrow sense, I feel uncomfortable. There are of course good ways and bad of doing anything. But I think the good ways are those least tied to any rigid system. No two gifted children are alike, physically or mentally, and it is the teacher's business to find out what suits each particular child. He must not impose a uniform drill on them all.

I am sure that teaching today is far more flexible and sympathetic than it was in my own early years. I am sure that we owe much of the astonishing ability of our best youngsters to the fact that they have been encouraged to develop their natural talents more freely and with less constraint. The best teachers I know are those whose pupils show the greatest variety of accomplishment and personality. The inborn gifts of the pupil are allowed to express themselves in ways most congenial, both physically and artistically, to the temperament and responsiveness of the individual. And it is from among these carefully nurtured young talents that there comes, from time to time, the exceptional genius which eventually reaches a mature and acknowledged mastery.

(from *Introduction to Celebrity Recital*, Solomon, BBC World Service, 17 May 1955)

Of Music and Musicians in particular

Some years ago I was able to look through seven or eight volumes
of music which had belonged to Jane Austen, including many songs
and pieces which she had copied out with her own hand. It was a
most interesting glimpse, both of Jane Austen's own musical taste
and of the fashions of domestic music a century and a half ago.

Many will know how unique Jane Austen was in giving vivid and
absorbing descriptions of quite ordinary people living ordinary lives
in the country houses of 150 years ago. Three or four families in a
village was all she needed to produce her masterpieces *Pride and
Prejudice, Sense and Sensibility* and the rest: novels which Sir Walter
Scott himself pronounced to be inimitable. Her music books were part
of the domestic life she lived, playing country dances for her nephews
and nieces, accompanying and no doubt singing simple songs. Printed
music was then neither cheap nor easy to get, and Jane made manuscript copies of her favourites. About 1796, at the age of 21, she
writes: 'I practise every day as much as I can', and later she says: 'I will
practise country dances that we may have some amusement'.

But although these simple accomplishments seem quite apart from
the intense imaginative life of a great writer, Jane's very pointed pen
shows itself occasionally, even when she writes about music. There
is one sentence in *Northanger Abbey* which I must quote. She is
describing her heroine Catherine Morland, who played the piano;
and she says: 'Though there seemed no chance of Catherine throwing
the whole party into raptures ... she could listen to other people's
performances with very little fatigue.'

'With very little fatigue' ... that is the incomparable Jane. And
beside that quiet irony you must put these music books, so devotedly
copied and practised. The music itself is interesting to a musician,
because it is nearly all contemporary and nearly all forgotten. One
or two bits of Handel and Haydn, but no Bach, Purcell, or anything
earlier. There is one piece by Mozart ascribed to someone else. Most

of it is by composers like Pleyel (a favourite pupil of Haydn, with 29 symphonies, 8 concertos and scores of quintets and quartets to his credit), and Schobert (a famous player of and composer for the harpsichord) who were fashionable then but have become almost completely forgotten since; and those composers who are still known to us are mostly known by other works. Dr Arne is a case in point. In his life-time he was an important composer of Grand Opera. The songs we know now, like 'Where the Bee sucks' and 'Blow, blow thou winter wind' were then considered the merest trifles. But these have lived and the operas are dead. He also wrote a great many cantatas, which were not what we now call cantatas, but dramatic or narrative scenes for a solo voice, accompanied. There are a great many quite simple songs in the books, by composers like William Shield, who began life as a boat-builder apprentice, took to the violin, led and wrote many operas, and finally became Master of the King's Music; and Charles Dibdin, who wrote 'Tom Bowling' and hundreds of other songs. He was a very gifted Southampton lad who came to London, kept a shop, acted, sang, wrote novels and a five-volume history of the stage, organised theatrical companies and wrote and produced many operas. Jane's copy of his *The Oddities* (a 'musical entertainment') is autographed by Dibdin ...

(Music-Lovers' Calendar, 28 May 1944)

Brahms's Clarinet Quintet

There are two main types of virtuoso. The most common is the performer who combines unusual facility with keen technical application and becomes an acrobat of the keyboard, or of the fingerboard, or of the vocal cords. All these have their place in the broad field of artistic endeavour, and some of them have made notable contributions to progress in a particular sphere. The acrobatics of one generation often become the accepted technical standards of the next.

Rarer, but far more important, are those artists who draw from their instruments a new aesthetic experience, who refine and enlarge the range of tone, who learn to devise and control new subtleties of phrasing, new varieties of expression, and who in fact create a new form of music by virtue of their mastery of the means of making it. Such men in our own time are Casals, Tertis, Léon Goossens. Each of these has raised his chosen instrument to a higher musical power, and each has stimulated both the study of the instrument itself and the production of music especially suited to it. The virtuoso has thus often preceded and influenced the composer.

Brahms's Clarinet Quintet is an example of this influence, for we owe it, and the other works of Brahms which employ a solo clarinet, to the pre-eminence of Richard Mühlfeld as a performer on that instrument. Brahms was greatly impressed by Mühlfeld's playing and was moved to write works which should be worthy of so distinguished a talent. And the clarinet is eminently suited for chamber music.

It is worth noting that there is also a Brahms Clarinet Trio, a Mozart Clarinet Quintet, and a Beethoven Clarinet Trio, all accepted as among the gems of chamber music. No other single wind instrument has been given such a distinguished repertory. And the reason is not far to seek. It lies in the character of the instrument itself, and in the succession of fine players who have mastered it.

The clarinet has a very large effective range, but this range varies in tone quality beyond that of any other wind instrument. It has an extreme flexibility of execution in the hands of a good player; and even average players, as in a military band, can make it take the place of the violin. Above all, its dynamic variety is unique, from a *pianissimo* hardly audible, to that piercing *fortissimo* which may explain its name − 'the little trumpet.' These qualities give it a peculiar fitness for combination with strings, because its soft tones, particularly in the lower registers, can be made to merge unobtrusively into that of the strings, while it is always ready, at any pitch, to produce a volume of tone that will stand out clearly and give to its part a characteristic definition and quality. All these virtues Brahms realised to the full, and his Quintet is not a solo plus a quartet, but a musical texture for five combined instruments, one of which is a clarinet.

The prevailing key is B minor, and this calls for two remarks. A sharp key is the proper medium for the clarinet in A, which is somewhat richer in tone, though less brilliant, than the clarinet in B flat. The clarinet in A also emphasises those more sombre colours which are characteristic of the lowest register of both instruments, and the extra semitone of compass downwards adds to this effect.

But the remarkable thing about the prevailing key of this Quintet is the degree to which it prevails. The first movement is naturally pivoted around B minor. The second movement is ostensibly in B major, but the harmonies often have a minor tinge, and the middle section is emphatically B minor. The third movement begins in D major, but the one definite modulation in the first section is to B minor. The second section (*Presto*) is a complete movement in B minor, which turns away to D major only at the end. Most remarkable of all in this respect is the last movement, consisting of a theme in B minor, three variations in B minor, one in B major, a fifth in B minor, and at the end a coda, borrowed from the first movement, again undisguised B minor. I know of no other work of this length which is so bound to one key.

And the thematic material is equally characteristic. The essence of a minor key is a minor third, and the falling minor third, D to B, might serve as a motto for the whole of this Quintet. It is behind one of the most pregnant phrases in the first movement. The material of the second movement is closely akin to it. The third movement, in both sections, uses it as a theme, while the melody of the last movement begins with the same inflection. These phrases are tabulated below:

This persistence, throughout a long work, of closely connected musical thoughts, a persistence both of key and of melodic inflection, suggests certain inferences. The unwavering pursuit of a fixed idea is characteristic of two types of mind − those which are poor in invention, and those which are profoundly sensitive. The composer without invention is not rare, but he is usually content to be a theorist, a technician, a teacher rather than a creator. The more creative mind generally suffers from having too many ideas rather than too few. That is why young writers give us a string of bright notions which seem to have no guiding plan. It is the setting of an idea which gives it significance. It is the mature mind which can see the deeper meanings in a simple phrase and can then marshal and control all the technique of the art in order to give that phrase its utmost purport.

That is what Brahms does in this Quintet, as in so many of his later works. He is completely master of a method, a technique, which has become part of himself — which we all feel to be uniquely and clearly the musical language of Brahms. This musical speech he uses to express and amplify an idea deeply conceived or a mood keenly felt. It is the music of an old mind, old in the sense that it has passed and conquered all the temporary and superficial artistic temptations, and can now pursue with unhurried yet unfailing intensity the beauty and significance of themes and thoughts which in themselves are merely germinal, which only show their true stature as he gradually invests them with the accumulated wealth and power of his mind and heart.

The later piano pieces are examples of this combined simplicity of ideas and maturity of handling. The falling third in this Quintet, than which nothing could be simpler as a melodic and musical theme, becomes in the course of the work more and more full of aesthetic meaning and distinction. You will perhaps remember those poignant falling thirds at the end of the last work Brahms wrote, the eleventh Chorale Prelude for the organ, which so closely preceded his death. That was Brahms in his inmost and ultimate maturity. There is something of the same mood, of the same final and consummate expression of a musical faith long nurtured and long cherished, in the simple themes which play so large a part in this Quintet.

There are four movements, of which the first is formally the most complex. But the architecture of this first movement is, except for one feature, quite orthodox and traditional. There is no introduction and there are no extraneous episodes. The first two bars contain a figure of six semiquavers (*see* Ex. 2) which is an important decorative 'point'

Ex. 2

in later sections of the movement. This figure strikes the 'Allegro' cast of the prevailing tempo. It is followed by two statements of (I) and then the string quartet subsides on to a chord of D major and the clarinet makes its entry, climbing softly up an arpeggio of this chord to take the lead in a repetition and extension of the first few bars. It is all quite captivating in its unerring sense of simple values, and one could go on analysing the whole textures line by line with equal profit.

But I want to deal in the main with the broader outlines. You can study the details in the score. Sonata or first-movement form, as it is generally understood, can be made to suffer badly in the aesthetic sense by too rigid a definition of its parts. The basic principle of the form is contrast, but it is often contrast by growth. It is in its origins a scheme of keys, a sequence of broad harmonic progressions, rather than a scheme of disparate themes. The distinct themes may be there, but it is their sequence and grouping in the harmonic sense which gives the movement its coherence, and hence its architectural unity. There is a group of ideas in the main key, and we are led by development and modulation to another group of ideas in another key. That is really all one can say in general terms of the exposition of a sonata-movement of classical form.

The turning point, as between the two groups, begins in this movement at bar 25 with the new theme:

Ex.3

By the time we reach bar 36 we are in the sphere of the main contrasted key, D major, and from that point to the double bar we have a whole group of ideas centring round that change of harmonic focus. There are many delightful effects, both of colour and emphasis, and one very Brahmsian phrase:

155

Ex. 4

which is closely akin to a phrase in the earlier B minor group.

The development section is remarkable for a lively interplay of fragments drawn from Ex. 2, and for a long *quasi sostenuto* treatment of the rhythm with which Ex. 3 begins. Above this are beautiful melodic fragments and long *cantabile* notes. Finally a lovely F sharp dominant pedal, against which is set a murmuring and falling duet of semiquavers between the clarinet and the 'cello, brings us back to the original key of B minor and to the initial group of ideas.

The recapitulation is for the most part exact, except that instead of the orthodox restatement of our second group in the key of the movement (B minor) Brahms gives us this group centred round a new harmonic pivot, G major. Then towards the end of the group he turns the logic of the harmonies in the direction of B minor again, and by a crescendo and climax which is the highest dynamic point of the movement prepares us for a quiet ending which fixes the final key and recalls the first group of themes. His last words are a moving restatement by the clarinet, in detached and falling fragments, of the phrase (I) which is so intimately expressive of his underlying mood.

II

It is generally conceded that a slow movement is a more exacting test of a composer's quality than a quick one. The excitement of rapidly recurring accents and stresses, the faster interplay of parts, the stronger contrasts of character and mood, all of which, given the necessary invention and energy, help to sustain the life and interest of an Allegro, have to be replaced by a deeper and more concentrated attitude of mind in an Adagio. A long slow melody is far more difficult to achieve than a lively and lilting tune. Time must be made to stop, or at least must be so overlaid by sheer beauty and intensity of thought that we cease to be conscious of it. The composer has to make

156

us content to accept a contemplative mood and to remain absorbed in it for comparatively long periods. His thoughts must therefore have an inherent quality which will bear the strain of a slow pulse and a gradual unfolding.

The first section of this slow movement (II*a*) is an ideal example of the technique of presentation applied to an expressive and slow-moving melody. The clarinet sings, the strings are muted, the first violin echoes the mood of the clarinet at a lower pitch and in a cross rhythm, the three lower strings play very simple ornaments around very simple harmonies. First violin and clarinet reverse their parts, and then the two violins in octaves, with the clarinet below or between them rise in wider phrases to the climax of the section. A few quiet and beautiful modulations, a return of the initial melody, an interrupted and then a final cadence, and that is all. It is very simple, and its values are of quality, not of quantity. And aesthetic quality, in music as in everything else, cannot be communicated in any terms other than its own. If we feel it we are content. If the thought or the language leaves us cold, there is no help for it. We are deaf to that particular message.

The middle section of this movement (see Ex. 5) is in some respects the most original part of the whole quintet. Here Brahms frankly devotes himself to using the more virtuoso-like capacities of the clarinet, and in providing a background for the clarinet's powers of execution and ornamentation he turns the string quartet into a miniature orchestra accompanying as it were, a miniature concerto:

Ex.5

The various devices of tremolo, the rich double-stopping, and the elaborate decoration, in all the parts, of harmonies which are in themselves simple in design — these are all characteristic of the virtuoso attitude of mind. This section is emotionally strong, too, and rises to a high climax. It begins and ends in B minor.

There follows a series of more recondite modulations which fall ultimately into B major and lead to a complete repeat of the first section. Then at the end we have one of those magical codas that Brahms knew so unerringly how to write. The strings are led to a *pianissimo* seventh, the clarinet remembers its decorative phrases (Ex. 5) of the middle section and suggests them in slower and more lyrical fashion, also *pianissimo*; the first violin echoes and then sinks with the other strings on to the final chord, through which the clarinet climbs by delicate arpeggios to a last falling third. It is at once one of the simplest and one of the most beautiful endings in all chamber music.

III

If one were asked which of the four movements of this Quintet has the most decidedly Brahmsian flavour one might well, on first thoughts, cite the first. That movement certainly bears the stamp of his mind unmistakably from beginning to end. But on second thoughts, I am not sure that the central and most important section of the third movement is not the best answer to this question. In that section we come very near indeed to an aesthetic problem which busied him always, and which brought him in his maturer years to a new conception of one of the main architectural features of a broad symphonic structure.

It is the problem of the Scherzo, and Brahms found new solutions of it. The lighter movements of Haydn and Mozart had been pure comedy, miracles of delicate, carefree, scintillating wit and humour in musical terms. Beethoven went further, much further. He could be humorous to the point of sheer boisterousness. His laugh was gigantic, his humour volcanic, his wit often near to a resounding practical joke. Brahms was made in another mould. The cast of his musical mind was always essentially serious. Pure comedy was not natural to him. Nor did he take to the musical practical joke. He was at the same time too serious and too fastidious for the conventional Scherzo of his predecessors. In the four symphonies there is only one true Scherzo — the

C major movement in number four. And opinion for a long time found even that one rather heavy-footed. If therefore Brahms had to accept the four-movement scheme in his extended works, and yet retain his own personal musical reactions, he had to invent either a new type of Scherzo or a new substitute for it. He did both.

You will find a number of these lighter movements among his Intermezzi and Capriccios. You will find, in the first three symphonies, three separate and different solutions of this same problem. And in the third movement of this Clarinet Quintet you see him producing yet another. I am speaking in particular of the long central section. It is playful, yet it is wistful. It rises at times to something approaching a rough boisterousness. But he cannot sustain either pure comedy or frank high spirits for long. There is delicacy, but it is pensive. There is vitality, but it is disciplined. There is wit, but it runs into poetry rather than into prose. The total result is something quite new in aesthetic tinge. It has the pace of a conversational comedy, but all the inflections are those of romantic verse. The very first little phrase sets the mood (III*b*). It is a happy stroke of wit, if you like. But its melodic essence is borrowed from a more serious source (III*a*).

The form of the whole third movement is highly symmetrical. There is a quiet little tune (III*a*) on the clarinet in D major, thinly harmonized by the viola and 'cello at first. Then the violins join in and the texture becomes richer:

Ex.6

The mood is easy and flowing. There is a *crescendo*, a sudden *piano*, a *diminuendo* and quiet ending in D.

Then, as if Brahms had said to himself: 'But this isn't a Scherzo at all,' we are carried suddenly off into what is going to be the mood of sustained playfulness, but of equally sustained wistfulness, which was Brahms's most charactristic reaction to the need for aesthetic lightness. Once the new theme is launched:

he must follow it generously. There is every kind of charming colour, and a regular second subject at bar 54 with its own expressive cadence in F sharp minor:

Ex.8

There is development of the sonata type, rising to high spirits after bar 100. Again a sudden *piano*, a *diminuendo*, and our first subject (Ex. 6) returns. Our second subject is recapitulated in orthodox fashion, even to the cadence in B minor. Then he recalls the development again as Beethoven might have done at the beginning of a symphonic coda. But Brahms feels that all this quick movement, spacious as it is, is only an interlude, as it were. And so he turns the harmonies towards D major, gives us another sudden *piano*, and a lovely last eight bars of the original quiet tune in D. Once more he has solved the Scherzo problem in a unique and characteristic way.

IV

Of the last movement little need be said. It is a simple melody, simply harmonized as a theme, with the first violin and the clarinet alternately stressing the prevailing inflection (IV). There are five variations, one in the major — but none of them strays far from the model. These are not variations like those of Beethoven's 'Diabelli,' or Brahms's own 'Handel,' where the theme is no more than a starting-point for a whole new creation of original ideas and moods which have only the very slightest direct allusion to the theme itself. The variations in this quintet are of the older type which we associate with Mozart or the early Beethoven. They are decorations of the theme. They neither supplant it, nor develop it beyond its own latent design. Only in the last variation do we meet a change of time-signature, 3/8 for 2/4, and this new form of the melody, played first by the viola, with the groups of semiquavers which from time to time ornament the texture, no doubt recalled to the mind of the composer the pace and atmosphere of his first movement. Once again, by the device of a *forte-piano*, we are led in a new direction, so far as the variation theme is concerned. But it is a frank return to the ideas with which the Quintet first began. The last thirty bars are in essentials quoted from the first movement. They are the coda to the whole work. They sum up and round off the thoughts which have constituted the prevailing mood of the Quintet. The falling cadence of the first movement is used again. Then a last *forte* chord, followed by a last *piano*; that is the end.
(A lecture delivered at the RCO, 16 Feb. 1935; printed in *The Musical Times*, April 1935)

Sibelius (i)

Jean Sibelius is by common consent one of the outstanding creative musicians of our time. Some of his admirers would place him among the great masters of all time. I shall not discuss this higher claim. All such contemporary judgments are at best pure prophecy, and at worst special pleading. No enthusiast can do more than attest his own experience and that of the society of like views with which he may be in contact. Personal verdicts of this kind are inevitably bound within narrow limits of time and place. Posterity

161

invariably modifies, and frequently reverses, the values of the past. What we call a great master is one whose work has survived this winnowing of the years and retained, through whatever ups and downs of opinion, an influence which many generations of men and many varied artistic fashions have yet agreed to account of permanent worth.

To acclaim a contemporary as one of the immortals is therefore an act of faith. The future may justify us, or it may condemn us. No one can forsee the ultimate standing of any new work of art, and the long historical chain of critical errors should teach us to beware of speaking beyond our brief. And there is a very real danger that in setting up a new idol we may be doing much less than justice to other and older faiths.

Sibelius himself has been the occasion of some curious critical verdicts. Those who will have him a great master forthwith, have been led to extol him by the too easy method of decrying his forerunners. Because Sibelius is great, we are told, therefore Wagner is not. Because the symphonies of Sibelius have certain convincing features, therefore the symphonies of Brahms, lacking these features, are to be held inferior. These are old tricks of advocacy, and time always explodes them. An artist is great, not by the limitations of his rivals, real or imagined, but by his own positive contribution to our experience. It will sufficiently stretch our powers to expound his own personal message. We have a thin case if we wander off into indiscriminate censure of other ideals and methods.

I shall therefore make no attempt to place Sibelius in any hierarchy, past or present. Nor shall I suggest that the music of Sibelius either destroys or displaces the catholic appreciation of other styles. What I hope to do is to indicate a few of those characteristic idioms of Sibelius which have for many of us a great and growing significance.

His life can be told in a few sentences. He was born in 1865 in a Finnish country town. His ancestry is both Swedish and Finnish. He did not turn to music as a career until he reached undergraduate age. He was in no sense a prodigy. He studied the violin and composition in Helsingfors, Berlin, and Vienna, and then returned home and taught at the conservatoire of Helsingfors from 1892 to 1897. He married a sister of the Swedish composer Järnefelt. At the age of 32 he had already so impressed his fellow-countrymen by his creative genius, that he was given an annuity by the State and was thereafter free to devote himself mainly to original work. It is now nearly forty years since this unique national tribute was paid to him. The rest of his life is a catalogue of his works, varied from time to time by visits abroad.

The number of his works is large, and their quality is very uneven. This is admitted even by his most staunch admirers, and we need not dwell on it. There have been some composers whose general level is very near their best. There have been others, and some of the greatest, who have written much that is merely competent, interspersed with works of glowing genius. Sibelius is one of these latter.

And even within the sphere of his finest compositions, Sibelius is not without certain fashions of speech which are occasionally not far short of mannerisms. He is very prone to particular melodic turns, to certain harmonic idioms, to a definite bias in his range of orchestral colours. These strokes can be of most arresting and convincing aesthetic purport. Sometimes they are, as it were, his signature on the pages of his poetic thought. He can be abrupt, stark and uncompromising beyond any composer known to us. He can also take and reiterate inflections and phrases which in other hands we account commonplace. He is not modern, in the narrower sense of that term. His vocabulary is mainly that of our classical traditions. Yet he can be angular and dissonant in a way that is all the more striking by virtue of its comparative rarity.

One other general characteristic of his best work should be remarked. Sibelius is a reaction, and a very uncompromising one, both from the fluent sentiment and from the technical opulence of the late 19th century. We all know how the romantic music of the 19th century was itself a revitalising reaction from the more conscious formalism of the 18th. Romance encouraged sentiment, sentiment in the lesser men became sentimentality. At the same time the actual apparatus of music was growing fast both in extent and competence. The orchestra offered an enormous range of new and richer colours. As late as a generation ago men were still apologising for the comparative austerity of Brahms. Wagner's orchestral palette had intoxicated the whole musical world and there was a universal demand for ever more and ever richer colours. Indeed at the beginning of our present century only the grandiose, the luscious, and the piquant had much hope of immediate fashionable acclaim.

Sibelius is remarkable if only for this, that the formative period of his life seems to have been almost totally uninfluenced by the prevailing currents that surrounded them. For forty years now he has been writing music which is a flat denial of the empty technique, the harmonic experiments and the orchestral parlour-tricks which have so often passed for genius in our concert halls. The slow progress of his reputation is a reflection of these facts. He wrote a few immediately attractive pieces which made his name known, but his major works were not so much condemned as ignored. The closest listeners were puzzled, the normal audience repelled. It is now thirty-five years since the second Symphony, twenty-five since the fourth. Of the latter work two of the most sensitive interpreters of our age, Toscanini and Beecham, have both confessed that only after a long time and many performances could they arrive at an executive understanding of such stark and concentrated idioms. Sibelius calls his music 'cold water'. It is often cold water in a north-east wind. It found its first appreciation in his own native sub-arctic land. It is not without significance that next to his own country he is now best understood in England. We too have our tonic east winds, and contrive to survive them. Only the comparatively genial fifth Symphony, written to mark his jubilee in 1915, has found much acceptance in Europe. The Sibelius Society is an English product.

Of the many positive ingredients which make Sibelius's music so distinctive I would put first his remarkable control of that fundamental background of time which governs all the processes of musical thought. We who teach and write about music dwell too exclusively on points of melody or harmony, on counterpoint or colour. Behind all these details is the crucial time-factor. A musical idea is significant only when it is convincingly related to that stream of time in which all music is immersed. The immature composer usually has too many ideas rather than too few. What he lacks is the instinct which prepares and controls, which can wait for the inevitable moment and can foresee a climax of interest without anticipating it. Of this process of controlled and relentless preparation Sibelius is a master. Some of his most characteristic habits are an integral part of it.

He is very fond of 'pedal' basses. For scores of bars in succession his basses will hold grimly to one note, with no more than a pulse to mark the passage of time. The bass broods, or crouches, one might say, until the vital change must come. He is very fond of long, sombre chords on the horns. These, too, will hold the music in leash for pages at a time. He has a habit of progressively silencing the rest of his orchestra and leaving the strings on a scarcely audible tremolo, which seems to begin nowhere, and which may wander uneasily through all kinds of vague figures and harmonies for fifty bars, until one begins to wonder when, if ever, this restless preparation will reach its goal. His little wisps of phrases on isolated wind instruments, sometimes faintly suggestive, sometimes stridently dissonant, often sound deliberately incongruous, and only after many statements and variations begin to show their latent musical significance. All these things are part of an iron control of the time-factor, which is to my mind the most impelling of Sibelius's gifts. Nothing can hurry him, nothing can divert him, until the precise moment comes towards which his mind is inexorably moving.

My own view of Sibelius is that we have in his scores a rare and possibly unique psychological document. Most composers of distinction have given us their ideas in mature and final form. They have selected and moulded their thoughts before recording them, and their leading themes, though they may have many adventures in the course of the work, are for the most part already fixed and complete before they are uttered. Of the formative processes of the mind which precede these utterances we have only one substantial record. Beethoven left us his sketch-books, and in these we can often trace an idea from its germ to its maturity. When I read a score of Sibelius I feel that I am not only being given the final product of a very remarkable and original thinker, but that he has contrived to record at the same time the actual formative processes of his mind. There are technical parallels in Henry James, Conrad, and Proust. Writing can of itself beget and define thought.

Sibelius often begins with the mere germ of a theme, sometimes so slight or so vague that nine composers out of ten would discard it. He may repeat a tentative phrase, and thus gradually emphasise its importance, or he may add to it, and as likely as not show us that the addition is the really significant part. Or after many turns of thought he may burst suddenly into something quite different, for which all that has gone before is only a setting. It is this unusual technique which makes it quite impossible either to foresee the form of his

165

movements or to guess which feature will ultimately provide the aesthetic climax. We are, I believe, following the actual development of his mind, as he creates, moulds, selects, and writes at the same time. The whole work may be complete in his thoughts before he puts pen to paper, but what he eventually writes includes the gradual process of creation. And to follow him thus is a highly vivid and stimulating experience.

Nothing is more difficult to describe in words than the emotional content of music. Yet here again we have in Sibelius a very original temperament, with a range and intensity of expression as remarkable as his method of presentation. The two aspects are really one, and you must go to the actual music to comprehend them. I will try to say something of my own feeling with respect to his aesthetic purport. He is generally described as by nature sombre, and this is broadly true. But it is not so much sadness as seriousness which is the prevailing tone. He can be genial, even gay, at times, and there is in him a good deal of whatever is the musical equivalent of serene yet slightly pungent humour. He can write frank, simple, and beautiful melody. But it is undoubtedly at the other end of the emotional scale that he is most original and most compelling.

He has pondered much on the folk-lore of his native land and is extremely sensitive to its wild surroundings, its forests and lakes, untrodden wildernesses and bleak northern plains. Many of his works are tone-pictures of these elemental forces and of the stark human dramas which the sagas of the north have fittingly placed in these settings. He is to my mind a man of that very rare temperament which can project itself into the most powerful and primitive emotions and yet retain a conscious control both of his own soul and of his chosen means of expression. We have had in recent years more than one composer who has affected an adopted barbarism, just as we have had many so sophisticated that they are incapable of feeling anything. Sibelius is rather the inspired tragedian, who can express to us the terror of Macbeth or the madness of King Lear, and yet do no violence to the controlled verse of Shakespeare.

In one respect I think Sibelius goes beyond any music I know. He reaches (I feel it particularly in the fourth Symphony) those depths of expression which are totally beyond words, and almost beyond music, even to suggest. Just as in the later Beethoven we sometimes feel that

166

music is reaching towards the ineffable, towards that transcendental region of the spirit of which music itself can only touch the outer confines, so through another facet of our emotional experience Sibelius gives us, I think, a glimpse of that elemental intensity of man's nature when he could as yet only feel and suffer a poignancy of emotion of which he was too dumb to speak. We sense, as it were, those deep and wondering caverns of the mind which existed before speech began.

The tense and cumulative method of his musical argument, and the abrupt manner in which he will bring it to a close, features which have puzzled many listeners, seem to arise spontaneously both from his powers of expression and from his strength of conviction. Having said his say, he has done. He cannot draw out a cadence or add a conventional peroration. He has no concern with niceties of form. He writes the naked truth as he feels it and then shuts the book. I sat beside a musical friend recently, listening to the fifth Symphony. You may recall that the second movement, whimsical, genial and beautiful as it is, ends by simply evaporating in two or three quiet chords and one very simple cadence. My friend said it sounded exactly as though Sibelius has come in and discussed a congenial subject, and then got up and said: 'Well, I think that's all. So long!'

The end of the first movement of that Symphony is equally characteristic. The movement as a whole is one long crescendo and accelerando of interest and intensity. It ends in a blaze of sound and at a breathless pace. The single bars are so fast that they fall into secondary groups of four. There is no slackening, no release, till we fall with the utmost emphasis on to a short final chord of E flat. And this chord is actually not on the first, but on the fourth beat of the prevailing group. It is as if one were flung with irresistible strength on to the pulse of the next first beat, which is not there! The true end is after the bar-line. It is a final stroke of complete silence.

The end of the last movement of this Symphony is equally striking and equally unique. Return is made to a broad melodic figure which in other hands might have been unbearably commonplace. Sibelius gradually invests it with a strength and with a nobility, both of inflection and harmony, which carry us to unforeseen realms of true and moving grandeur. There is an inexorable march of thought which drives the music through many strange chords, and with ever

167

increasing intensity, to a goal which, when we reach it, is the pure 'tonic and dominant' of our forefathers. We have arrived at last at the culmination of the whole work, a final confession of faith in the fundamental verities of our symphonic heritage. And then come suddenly the last six detached and crashing chords, all quite simple in themselves, but so widely spaced in time that one holds one's breath for the next. The last but one is a plain dominant, the last a plain tonic, both in unison and fortissimo. It is as if a great thinker, having pursued a long and unbreakable chain of argument, should at last reach a final truth, state it in the strongest and simplest terms, and then add the old formula: *Quod erat demonstrandum.*

I would like to say a word regarding the external influence of Sibelius, as I see it. I do not think he can found a school. His speech is so personal that to imitate it is to risk a caricature. Nor are there any prevailing forms that might become fertile conventions for the future. He may well remain an isolated figure, however great his repute may grow.

But he has done at least two things of very high value. He has blown a breath of fresh and purifying air through the overheated corridors of contemporary experiment. And he has definitely enlarged the emotional range of music, without destroying any of the accepted foundations on which that art has hitherto been built. He has shown us that it is not a new speech that we need. What we need is something vital to say, and the skill, courage and sincerity wherewith to say it.

(A lecture, with musical illustrations, delivered at Leeds University, 12 October 1936; printed in *The Musical Times*, November 1936)

Sibelius (ii)

The career of Sibelius is in some ways more remarkable than that of any of his contemporaries. Born in the comparatively small but highly cultured society of Finland, his devotion to its natural beauty and heroic history was matched by his country's appreciation of him. His First Symphony was written in 1899 and owed something to Russian predecessors. But in his Second Symphony (1902) there was an unmistakably personal and original speech, and the five symphonies which followed in the next twenty years have each of them been quite unique, neither imitating each other nor following any approved pattern, past or present. And he has contrived to be arrestingly original without any forced stretching of the traditional bounds of melody or harmony. He does not need either a new scale or new chords. He does not eschew simple fragments of tune or the normal logic of harmony. What he does is to select these elements and give a setting and significance so vivid and compelling that they have the force of a new discovery. And his architectural sense is equally novel and powerful.

His orchestral scoring is by nineteenth-century standards stark and sombre. Here, too, he needs no new instruments nor any orchestral virtuosity for its own sake. His mind has long dwelt on the landscape and legends of the hardy north, and this spirit is reflected in many musical poems, of which the epic *Tapiola* (1925) is the last and greatest. He portrays at once the force of nature and the virility of man. His influence and stature have grown steadily, particularly in England, and he has been especially admired by the younger men, not so much as a model for imitation, but as representing a healthy contrast to the over-complex and over-delicate alike. He has, moreover, proved that when men are inclined to complain that poetry can go no further, it is the poets that are exhausted, not the language.

(from Hadow's *Music*)

Elgar

In the year 1900 Elgar was forty-three years of age, Puccini forty-two, Debussy and Delius thirty-seven, Richard Strauss thirty-six, and Sibelius thirty-five. These were the men who dominated the first decades of the century. Elgar had written his *Enigma* Variations, the first work by an Englishman displaying complete mastery of modern orchestral technique. His *Dream of Gerontius* was produced in 1900. By the standards of that time it was difficult, and it had to grow slowly into favour. But by this oratorio, as new and personal as it was masterly and sincere, Elgar added one more to the comparatively few choral masterpieces which have increased in stature and breadth of appeal with every year that has passed. *The Apostles* and *The Kingdom* followed in 1903 and 1906, and his two symphonies in 1908 and 1911. Elgar's style has founded no school. His frank emotion, opulent scoring, spacious architecture, and wealth of decoration were

169

the climax of an epoch that has gone. During his later years the younger generation was already in revolt. But distance is gradually giving us an impressive perspective. The Edwardian pomp and grandiloquence which repelled the reformers is now seen in a far mellower light. There was behind it the solid belief in an established order which we now recall somewhat wistfully. We begin to appreciate that stability we can no longer command. And we find it implicit in Elgar, the consistent faith, powerful invention, secure poise; and if that poise was aristocratic, well, Elgar was an aristocrat in music, and his symphonies are the monuments of a society that tried to live spaciously and, when the testing time came, was ready to respond nobly.

(from Hadow's Music)*

Delius

... The position of Frederick Delius in contemporary opinion is a curious one. He is no longer young, his mature work has been published and has been heard in bulk, and he has without any doubt completely assimilated an original and an essentially modern technique in terms of a consistent level of thought. He has gained an almost universal respect, even from those to whom his particular angle of vision is not altogether sympathetic. There are some who consider the body of his work as a whole to be not only masterly as a means of expression, but unfailingly beautiful in its results. A few there are who hail him as incomparably the greatest musician of our time, though this opinion is sometimes urged with an impatience which to some extent defeats itself. Yet it is impossible to deny that the general appreciation of Delius is far from secure. In England he had an able and devoted missionary in Sir Thomas Beecham, who gave his work that practical support which is worth more than any number of literary advertisements. The movement thus admirably inaugurated has not held its ground. It is said that we are too stupid or too inept to understand Delius; that he is better appreciated abroad. This may be so, though if the number of performances of his works given on the continent be divided by the number of

---

* Dyson revised this work for a 1949 O.U.P. reprint, adding a chapter on 20th-century music from which these excerpts are taken.

orchestras and choruses available, not to mention the number of opera-houses, England may not emerge from the comparison so incorrigible a sinner as might at first sight appear. We are certainly no worse than Paris, to say the least. No, the present reputation of Delius is a phenomenon not of our locality, but of our time. How far has he himself contributed to it? He is not aggressively an innovator, yet he distinctly belongs to the modern school. He seems indeed to represent, among the many crudities and exuberances of experiment, that ideal mean which should appeal to a similar level of public appreciation. Where lies the fault?

In the first place, Delius has written little or nothing for the piano, or for those small combinations of instruments which are a very potent factor in the contemporary dissemination of music. There are admirable piano arrangements of most of his works, but they have to be read or played with imagination. His peculiar values, his essentially orchestral economy, suffer greatly when divorced from their proper medium. He also makes formidable demands on the technique of performance, on the understanding, and on the aesthetic sensibility of listener and performer alike. If one is not alert enough to listen, Delius will not periodically surprise one into wakefulness. He has no facile tricks, no seductive emotionalism, no nervous intoxication to offer. Neither is he telling a raw tale, nor cracking jokes. He is not overcome with a sense of his own technical capacity. All is not grist to his mill. There are many things now fashionable which he does not, will not, say. Complaint is sometimes made that there is so little one can carry away, so to speak, from Delius. But how much can one carry away, in this sense, from an unfamiliar work by Bach? Delius has a melodic gift, but it is usually rhapsodic. He has an amazing harmonic instinct, but it is diffused. He does not distil his thought into a single line, nor into a striking passage. Delius is concerned primarily with texture, just as Bach was. It is a sustained atmosphere that he seeks, and texture is his approach to it. His method is harmonic; Bach's was contrapuntal. But however fundamental this divergence may be technically, and however much one may doubt whether, so long as we think and play our parts horizontally, the more disparate impressions of harmony can hope to rival the sustained perfection of melodic counterpoint, this does not alter the fact that texture as such has aesthetic values of its own which may be derived neither from those of the single line nor yet from the reflected light of powerful harmonic themes. We do not demand from Bach the values either of Mozart or of Wagner. Delius learnt his art away from the schools, away from the fashions of his day. His diction has in it a tinge of aloofness, even of vagueness, which to some temperaments is a real difficulty. But he has at least one quality which is perhaps above all others scarce in our time; he has a deep, a quiet, and an intrinsic sense of beauty. Is it this that our generation has lost or is losing? His idylls *On hearing the first cuckoo in Spring* and *Summer night on the river*, and a dozen other movements of tranquil yet enchanted fantasy, were not born of the tumult of to-day. Like the idyll of Siegfried, they must be tasted without passion, without impatience. Delius is not of the market-place. So homogeneous is he that it is sometimes hard to tell where folk-song ends and Delius begins. It is hard to tell where is melody and where harmony. His is often a rhapsodic art, but still more is it at times an art of pure contemplation. And an art of pure contemplation is not easy to practise in this twentieth century of ours.

(from *The New Music*)

Vaughan Williams (i)

... Far from being precocious, Vaughan Williams was notably the reverse. He studied under many masters and he steeped himself in folk-music and in the Tudor and Purcellian traditions, but he was already thirty-seven years old when the song-cycle *On Wenlock Edge* and the string *Fantasia on a Theme of Tallis* first showed how deep and how original was his genius. These were followed in the next year by the *Sea Symphony*, a work he at once revised, and which has now become a choral classic. Since then he has written five symphonies, the latest being produced while these lines are being written. The second portrayed, on a large orchestral canvas, some of the teeming variety of life and the misty grandeur of London. The third is a unique Pastoral and the quintessence of the composer's intuitions of reflective beauty. The fourth jumped suddenly into the strident dissonances and vehemence of its period (1935). The fifth returns to euphony and the composer's characteristic love of weaving old inflexions into a new synthesis. The sixth is an epitome of our age, ending with a question-mark.

172

Of his many choral works since the *Sea Symphony* the apocalyptic *Sancta Civitas* is the most original and compelling. He has written three full-scale operas, none of them wholly successful, though they abound in beautiful music. He is in a sense too musical for the stage. He cannot sacrifice the continuity of his thought to the sudden contrasts and interruptions of dramatic action. He is at his best in the short operas in one mood, *Riders to the Sea* and *The Shepherds of the Delectable Mountains*, which combine fine poetry, restrained action, and the enveloping atmosphere of reflective music. Shorter works like *Flos Campi* and *The Lark Ascending* evoke this same contemplative intimacy. His Masque for Dancing, *Job* (1930), displays every facet of his genius, and has brought to the art of ballet a quality never before reached in that form. The story of Job as reflected in the pictures of Blake is a panorama of human destiny that could be fittingly matched only by music of the deepest significance. Every scene is of surpassing moment, and there is not in our whole musical literature a more moving and ennobling portrayal of human peril, steadfastness, and faith. These diverse fruits of the art of Vaughan Williams are a summation of the better tendencies and aspirations of our time. They explore, but with a profound sense of direction. They cover the whole range of musical poetry, and touch every worthy aspect of human hopes and fears. They are founded on an abiding faith in the spiritual power of an artistic creed unswervingly held and applied.

(from Hadow's *Music*)

Vaughan Williams (ii)

Creative artists can be divided into three classes. The majority have no marked originality, but they can produce competent work swiftly and reliably. They have a natural and spontaneous flair for the ideas and craftsmanship of their period. Their generic name in music is *Kapellmeister*, and the seventeenth and eighteenth centuries were full of them, because music then circulated only slowly and with difficulty, and the *Kapellmeister* had to compose as well as perform the music required by the church, the court, or the theatre which he served. The *Kapellmeister* of genius became a Bach, a Handel, or a Haydn.

A second class appears to be born with this complete technical

173

facility and adds to it an unceasing flow of original and infectious ideas. Mozart, Schubert, and Chopin were of this class. So was Richard Strauss yesterday, and so is Benjamin Britten today.

But there is a third and still rarer class of composers who seem when young to be endowed neither with technical ease nor particular distinction of idiom. Beethoven was one of these. So was Wagner. In our own day Sibelius might be placed in this category. Vaughan Williams is emphatically one of them, for no composer of comparable rank was so slow to mature. If any of these men had died at the age of Schubert, their names would have been obscure or unknown. Vaughan Williams at thirty was still a very uncertain student, groping for a musical language of his own.

Composers of this calibre are a most interesting study. They have a passionate desire to express themselves, and an unswerving strength of will which makes them persevere through a long struggle. Either their creative urge is so original and powerful that they must, like Beethoven and Wagner, burst through the conventions of their time or, alternatively, like Sibelius and Vaughan Williams, they must find a new and personal grammar of ideas congenial to their own distinctive thoughts and emotions. This process is inevitably gradual, and it must have behind it an unfailing imaginative purpose. Technique for its own sake does not exist for them. They have something new to say, and must find a way to say it by hard mental exploration.

This is why, I believe, Vaughan Williams did not really find himself until he was long past the normal student age. Since then every succeeding work has at once widened and consolidated his genius. We have now over forty years of subsequent creative work from him, and the end is not yet. In our era only Sibelius has shown so unswerving an aim, only Verdi such octogenarian fertility.

The point at which he reached, in my opinion, his characteristic height was when, at forty-five, he produced that unique 'Masque for Dancing': *Job*. There is in this work the whole essence of his musical thought. And as the story of Job is an epitome of man's pilgrimage from joy to sorrow, and from sorrow to humility, so does the composer's music illustrate the whole range of his creative and imaginative expression, his pleasure, his pathos and his faith. He had not only found his language, but he had learnt to command and expand it to the measure of his own deep and abiding ideals.

174

Job is also important because it was a turning point in his accepted repute. It was this work which confounded and converted many of those who had been most critical or lukewarm towards him. Those of us who can remember what the would-be 'smart' writers used to say of his earlier works can best follow him (and spare them) by forgetting those singularly mistaken estimates of his rank. The fact is that Vaughan Williams, like some of the great masters of the past, has always been in process of becoming; becoming more and more himself, and at the same time gathering slowly but permanently the ever-widening allegiance both of his fellow-musicians and of the musical public which he and they alike serve.

Today his eminence is secure, and no small part of it has its roots in the close connection he has preserved with the amateur friends and music-lovers of his own neighbourhood at Dorking. He has never become remote or estranged from the lives and intuitions of those who live in a typically English countryside and town. Hence his universality. He has felt, portrayed, and crystallised a long lifetime of human adventure and experience. There are in his works movements of every emotional complexion, from the fragrant simplicity of 'Linden Lea' to the prophetic dissonances of the Fourth Symphony. There is the broad human sweep of the *Sea Symphony* and the apocalyptic vision of *Sancta Civitas*, the nostalgic yearning of *Flos Campi*, and the innocent serenity of *The Lark Ascending*. He is for us, and to a degree unparalleled in our musical community, Everyman's composer.

(*Radio Times*, 12 June 1953)

Vaughan Williams (iii)

V.W.'s supreme rank in the creative music of our time needs no emphasis. I will write rather of his day-to-day generosity and friendliness. He was at one time a member of the Council of the Royal College of Music, but as our statutes debar members of the council from being members of the professorial staff, he at once resigned when Sir Hugh Allen asked him to take a few pupils in composition, and he taught for many years. Then, in 1939, when the war reduced our numbers by half, he immediately offered his class to colleagues whose work was most seriously depleted.

He was instantly ready to support from his own purse the many appeals, professional or otherwise, that came to him. Indeed it was sometimes difficult to persuade him that some causes were more deserving than others. His instinct was to help first and judge later, a trait of character occasionally too optimistic, but always endearing. He would go far to assist a promising talent or an enterprising programme.

His modesty could be embarrassing. I had great difficulty in persuading him to sit for Sir Gerald Kelly's magnificent portrait, now in the College council-room. He took the whimsical attitude that if you want a good portrait the subject of it is immaterial. If you want a good likeness, why not a photograph? Luckily we got both.

One last reminiscence. Not long ago he wrote to me describing a most vivid dream in which he heard some unknown music. He was told, in the dream, that I had written it, and he actually copied out a musical quotation from it! I could not recognize it, but I am more than content to have been given that fleeting moment in a unique imagination. [*The letter referred to is reproduced on p.   . Ed*].

(*Musical Times*, October 1958)

Charles Villiers Stanford (i)

To commemorate, for readers of this Magazine, the great gifts and the unique personality which have now passed into the history of our College, is a task which no one of us could approach without diffidence. The barest record would involve the experience of a dozen generations of students, each of whom saw Stanford from its own angle, and from each of whom a tribute would be due. Nor would even this represent, with anything approaching completeness, the impress of his work on our art as a whole. A yet broader vision of time is necessary, if Stanford's place in it is to be properly understood.

Some of us felt his power in early days, when he was in truth fighting for the very existence of what we now call the English renaissance. Some, like myself, came to him when the fight was virtually won, when he was without question one of the outstanding figures of his time, both in accomplishment and in recognition. Some saw him only when by the march of years his vigour had begun to wane, when it was not so easy to realise what a valiant protagonist he had been. But all of us, whether we knew him early or late, have inherited an English music whose unchallenged vitality we owe to the men of Stanford's generation. And among those men he was, by universal acclaim, one of the great captains.

It was in the seventies and eighties of the last century that Stanford's leadership was won, and it is difficult for us to imagine the environment which then afflicted music in England. There were still thousands of amateurs, not undiscriminating in other spheres, who seemed to hold that there was little music so admirable as that of Mendelssohn, and none better. Handel had a firm place in the public esteem, but of contemporary favourites Gounod, and his still shallower imitators, hardly misrepresented the prevailing taste. In such an atmosphere Stanford had the temerity to preach Schumann, to discover Brahms. Think of a London in which the classics appeared only intermittently. Native energy was mainly confined to a few provincial festivals, magnificent indeed, but necessarily available only for the few. Think of what passed for music in so many of the churches of that time. Think of the abysmal taste of the drawing-room. Remember to what trifling ends were directed the talents of many who had specifically musical gifts; virtuosities almost incredibly childish; weird names and weirder manners accounted the natural concomitants of artistic pretensions. So far as our national life was concerned, good music was still in the main an imported exotic, towards which the normal Englishman reacted sometimes with wonder, sometimes with scorn. The memory of Stanford demands from us the truth about these things.

And then turn to the years in which his life has closed. Is there more or better music now to be found anywhere than in London? Is there a village in England which has not to some extent followed his lead? Everywhere there is activity, much of it devoted to the highest ideals. It is music produced by Englishmen for Englishmen, and an increasing proportion of it is written by Englishmen too. It is confined to no place, nor to any class. A whole public school can join in the B minor Mass. There is practically no limit to the music that is now welcomed as a natural field for discrimination and training. Need one say more? This is the movement of which Stanford was one of the pioneers. These are the things he fought for. Towards the furthering of these things his life was spent. 'Si monumentum quaeris, circumspice.'

That his character had its angles, his enthusiasm its bounds, it would be a poor tribute to his memory to deny. Nor need we here urge on the other side his watchfulness and his essential kindliness, qualities which made him sometimes more like a parent than a master. Stanford was, like all effective reformers, a man of direct and uncompromising mould. What he believed, he believed, and there was an end of it. But it is difficult to see how with a spirit less fiery he could have done what he did. There had always been in England a number of comparatively cloistered souls, who had practised their art as they understood it, with modest integrity. Stanford challenged the continental giants on their own ground. He was to show the slow-moving public that it was possible to be a musician of pronounced distinction, and yet lose not a particle of one's native character. The very qualities which made him seem blunt and imperious in later years were just those which in earlier days had impressed an ever-widening circle of disciples. He had succeeded by force of character, by refusal of compromise. He never forgot his crusades. And he retained to the end something of the outward asperity of a partisan.

One of the most illuminating traits in his character was his reaction towards Wagner. He reminds one of an analagous fortitude in Samuel Butler. Just as Butler would not be coerced by the pontifical Darwinians, not because he misunderstood them, but because he understood them too well, so Stanford refused to be stampeded into the fashions of Wagnerianism. Many things in Wagner's art were frankly antipathetic to him. It was not insensitiveness, but the reverse. And who shall say that Stanford's own music would have been improved by the admixture of an atmosphere or of a technique so completely alien to his own natural intuitions? Stanford held to his own native strain. He gave it form and distinction. And it now has a permanent place in our history because he found some things good, and other things less good, and made no secret of the matter.

This integrity and these compact ideals were unsparingly devoted to the College. In some departments, and for a long period, he was virtually an autocrat. He covered practically the whole field of orchestral music, and he had the best traditions of classical interpretation at his fingers' ends. He was largely responsible for the production of a long series of operas, prepared without a theatre, and with so little stage rehearsal that only a strong faith and a ready improvisation could have produced them at all. He was not a virtuoso conductor. Virtuosity of every kind was alien to his temperament. Contrasted with the more exuberant, his methods appeared to be sound rather than inspired. But he could handle large masses with a command and with a dignity which revealed the nobility of masterpieces. And there was probably no man in England who better knew what one may call the 'shop' of the classics, the detail that scholars had fought over, the idiosyncracies of rendering ascribed to famous men of the past. Here he equalled the best men on the Continent, to whom such knowledge comes by direct inheritance. And this intimacy of understanding he could pass on to those whose taste was sufficiently keen.

As a teacher he naturally displayed both the virtues and the limitations of his temperament. He was impatient, blunt, and frankly hostile to much of what we are pleased to call modernity. To him music was, as it were, a body of truth, and what was not true was false. To deny the truth was heresy. To be lukewarm was to betray one's poverty of soul. Yet his technical advice was impeccable. And though few of his ablest pupils could embrace his particular dogmas, the best of them caught from him the stimulus of a faith of some kind, without which there can be little strength or merit in work. There has certainly been no other teacher of composition in England who has approached Stanford in the number and distinction of his pupils. If to be a great teacher is to produce neat samples after one's own model, then Stanford failed. If the proper criterion is an inculcated virility of speech, a sustained harvest of decided and coherent personalities, then Stanford was phenomenal in his success. This same bias was apparent in his own works. Youthful iconoclasts respected rather than emulated them. But those of us who played, from manuscript or from first proof, works like the *Songs of the Sea*, the *Irish Rhapsodies*, the *Stabat Mater*, or *Much Ado*, gathered, it is to be hoped, something of his essential cleanliness of thought, his directness of aim, his economy of expression.

Stanford's artistic philosophy was in essence an identification of music with everything he accounted best in the life of his place and time. Precious attitudes and artificial segregations he abhorred. The flowing locks or the queer clothes, which too often marked the social hybrid, met with scant courtesy in his presence. Music in England should wear, so to speak, the costume of the country, cloth cap and tweeds. It must not wilt before the east wind. Stanford began by proving that he could be a musician and an undergraduate. He went on to show that he could be a musician of outstanding quality and at the same time a characteristically normal member of English society. And those of us who have moved about the world and have heard men talk about our College as an institution, will agree that what the best men say of it is that no artistic school in the country can pride itself on a more convincing social sanity. This we owe to men like Grove, like Parry, like Parratt, like Stanford. It was the wealth of their connections with every department of English life and thought which enabled them to give to music a firm root in the structure. Stanford's versatility was immense. He was a composer, a conductor, a teacher and a writer, to an extent to which there are few parallels. It is possible that in some ways he was even too prodigal of his talents. A narrower or more selfish aim might have intensified his fame in a chosen direction. But whatever he touched he invested with a natural health, and it is not for us to regret his bounty. Our music is what it is to-day, in no small measure, because Stanford spent himself royally in covering the whole field of it.

(RCM Magazine, Easter 1924)

Charles Villiers Stanford (ii)

I was a pupil of Stanford for four years. I have more to thank him for than I can attempt to catalogue. But of his particular approach to the art of teaching, the subject with which I am here to deal, it is not easy to write.

I remember a good many of his characteristic explosions. I happened once to bring into his room a book or a paper in which he came upon a photograph of Gladstone. He leapt at it. 'Look at his face, my boy! Sinister, sinister in every line. Ugh!' Thus Stanford the Orangeman. Another day I heard part of a lesson given to a student who has since become famous. 'Blank,' he said, 'your music comes from hell. From *hell*, my boy; H E double L.' Thus Stanford the purist. Once he suddenly observed that my nose was obstructed. He took particular pains to have me examined gratis by a Harley Street specialist; and I know he did the like for others, too, who seemed to be ailing or disabled in any way. From another angle he once said to me: 'I want to talk to you, my boy. Don't spend too much time with So-and-so. He'll do you no good. I'd rather see you with a painted lady.' All his judgments were of this uncompromising type. When we were preparing *Tod und Verklärung*, he remarked: 'If it's to be Richard, I prefer Wagner. If Strauss, then give me Johann.' And after the performance at Queen's Hall of a famous work which to him seemed to smack too much of the hothouse, he is said to have relieved his discomfort in the artist's room by playing scales of C major. He once gave me a similar douche in a terminal report. 'Has a bad fit of chromatics. Hope he will soon grow healthy and diatonic.' At the end of my time with him I became Mendelssohn Scholar. 'What are you going to do with it?' he asked me when next we met. My ideas were vague, but I said something about Leipzig. 'No,' he answered, 'you've had four years here. That's enough. You don't want any more of that sort of thing. Go to Italy, my boy, and sit in the sun.'

I have set down these disjointed memories thus at random, because to me they represent him as no carefully chosen adjectives could do. This done, there comes the main question. Was Stanford a great teacher?

In the sense in which it is customary to understand the term, I think Stanford's teaching had most of the major defects that teachers are usually counselled to avoid. The careful exposition of principles, the weighing and collating of detail, the conscientious or laboured endeavour to understand or appreciate an alien or repellent point of view; these faculties had no sure place within his temperament. He could give first-rate technical advice. 'Keep the double-basses up.' 'Percussion is effective inversely in proportion to the amount of it.' 'You don't make more noise by scrubbing at a fiddle than by bowing it normally.' Remarks of this kind came frequently, and were invariably sound. But in matters more elusive, in questions of personal expression, of poetic or dramatic mood, of all the more modern devices of emphasis or atmosphere, he seemed to some of us to be a bundle of prejudices. His judgments in these things were so impatient, brusque and final. If he disagreed with a student's choice of a poem, he was not likely to find much sense in the setting of it. Sometimes his distaste was strong enough to defeat itself. The pupil might become sullen and the teacher bitter.

Something of this feeling of unresolved conflict seemed to lie behind the disappointment which in later years he occasionally confessed. He had aspired to be the acknowledged fount of a school of composers. In his own judgment he had largely failed. And this in spite of the patent fact that an overwhelming majority of contemporary English composers of distinction were his pupils. In proportion as these men developed a novel or personal speech, Stanford seemed to think that they were abjuring just those ideals which he had tried to instil. The ultimate products baffled or distressed him. His mature idol had been Brahms. To his pupils it too often seemed that what he wanted from them was Brahms and water. And hardly any of his most talented students could abide the mixture. It is said that some of them occasionally concocted a deliberate imitation in order to please him. Some certainly wrote in the knowledge that they would be condemned from the first bar. In a certain sense the very rebellion he fought was the most obvious fruit of his methods. And in view of what some of these rebels have since achieved, one is tempted to wonder whether there is really anything better that a teacher can do for his pupils, than drive them into various forms of revolution.

Stanford's real and abiding influence lay in qualities of mind and character of which he was probably never even conscious. His fundamental reactions were fierce and intuitive. There were some things to him so elemental that they rarely required to be expressed, much less argued about. And on this plane he carried most of his pupils with him, without their being in the least alive as to what was actually happening. Vagueness, shallowness, sentimentality, froth, and a score of other temptations to which every talent, young or old, is subject, were simply outside his orbit. They could not exist in his presence, and men left them outside his door like a coat or a hat. This was the real infection. His direct judgment, his tightness of speech, his fury of integrity, these were what he gave to those who could digest them. It was an influence as indirect as was the breadth and scholarship of Parry. One did not have to know Parry. He had only to sit in the Director's room at the Royal College, and it was impossible for slack or superficial work to feel at home there. How could an institution be aimless that had Parry at its head? How could a composition be meaningless vapour that had Stanford at its heels?

It was his passion for the artistic faith of his maturity which was the outstanding feature of his work. Something of this he had to pass on, and he did not fail. There is not, to my knowledge, a single one of his pupils who, having talent to do better, has chosen the easy path. To the ablest of them the facile, the imitative, the popular, the best-seller, are completely unknown. Not a few have been content to dig hard and long, to mould with not a little of Stanford's own ruggedness, such metal as they were able to find in themselves. Stanford had an encyclopaedic knowledge of music, and this alone was a notable experience to those who came in contact with it. He had also been in close touch with all the finest traditions and all the most gifted exponents of his time. And he was, as I have already shown, something of a true father to us all. But above all he had within him a refining fire, hidden it may be, but never quenched. As was lately said of a great headmaster whose outward manner was difficult: 'When all is done and said, the man cared.' Stanford cared, and cared passionately, for the art in which he lived. And if any of us, his pupils, have even a spark of that same fire, then, whether we know it or not, we burn it in his honour.

(Music & Letters, July 1924)

W.H. Reed

Dr. Reed was in his place at the luncheon table of the Royal College until Tuesday, June 23, 1942. That night he went to Scotland to hold examinations. He examined until Thursday morning, July 2, when, after hearing the first few candidates, he collapsed suddenly and died within a few minutes, at St. Joseph's College, Dumfries.

I have tried, while memory is both fresh and poignant, to jot down some slight impression of his unique personality, as it charmed and delighted my table at the Royal College almost daily for the last five years. If what I have written can recall to his friends, even family, a memory of that sparkling talk and those fine and generous ideals which are his legacy to us all, I shall be more than satisfied.

G.D.
The Royal College of Music,
8 July, 1942.

He held positions of great responsibility, he had many public successes and many honours, but through them all he was known affectionately and universally as 'Billy.' He was Billy to Elgar, who gave him, beyond anyone else, his artistic and personal confidence. It was Billy who first saw and heard many of Elgar's sketches. It was Billy who phrased and moulded some of those glowing musical thoughts. It was Billy's sympathy, skill, and ripe musical judgement which Elgar often sought when ideas were germinating.

It was this same Billy who would welcome a quite elementary and diffident young student, and devote untiring care and the most kindly criticism to any germ of talent, without impatience and without stint.

And it was Billy who throughout his life was instantly at ease with any keen group of amateurs, ready to lead, encourage and instruct, until he made a motley group of very unequal players into a coherent and hardworking orchestra. He never fretted, he never flagged. No artist of his rank has ever been more generous, less self-centred.

For he was an artist, and a great artist, through and through. He chose to become an orchestral leader, though his solo-playing was of a very high order. He fell into the place of leader because he had just those qualities on which other men rely. He loved team work, and his skill, his resilience, his speed of thought, and his encyclopaedic knowledge and memory, made him prominent whether he would or no. He began as a lad at the back desks. He became for a generation the finest leader of his time. He stood behind every conductor who had the good fortune to find him, whether that conductor were a giant or a fumbler. He held his orchestral team together, with superb results under a great conductor, with uncanny readiness and skill under a poor one. He saved orchestras, soloists, choirs and audiences from a thousand mishaps. He could lead *Ein Heldenleben* under Richter or Nikisch, and play that virtuoso solo-part with consummate mastery. He could visit some little provincial society and pull both the conductor and the players through every difficulty and uncertainty.

He was a peculiarly British product, because he lived through a peculiarly British period, when we were feeling our way towards new orchestral and musical standards. His life and his experience were an embodiment of that gradual change. He had great gifts, both technical and creative, as a composer. As a young man he was for a time one of the most fertile and promising of the younger school, and to the end of his days he wrote occasional works in which beauty, vitality and skill were fragrantly blended. But he was too versatile, too companionable, to cultivate a purely personal talent in conscious isolation. He was happiest in the rough and tumble of busy music-making, in the society of friends and fellow-musicians. And if, as may well be, we lost thereby a great solo artist, or a more personal and creative musical utterance, we gained a life of practical service, and a character which greatly influenced and raised the quality of our appreciation and the range of our standards. We were privileged to feel the effect of a personality in which selfless devotion, perfect skill, unfailing generosity, and gay humour were singularly combined.

The changes through which Billy lived, and of which his own career was an essential part, were quite fundamental, so far as the standards of concerted music were concerned. When he, then little more than a boy, began to play in the various London professional orchestras, they were hardly more than casual collections of good individual players, who came together for one or two particular occasions. Two rehearsals, perhaps, under whatever conductor had been engaged, in order to read through the programme and correct the more obvious errors of performance, then the public concert, and that was all. The same orchestra, in all its personnel, might never meet again, or only after a long interval. Symphony concerts were comparatively few, were special events, and no player could live on them.

Orchestral players lived by playing nightly in theatres and music-halls, and their outlook and discipline tended to be of that order. Often a good player was in two or three theatre bands at once. This was the cause of the almost universal 'deputy' system. A good flautist, for example, would be engaged for two theatres. It was quite understood that he could not be in two places at once, and he might even from day to day be playing at neither. But he was responsible for providing an adequate deputy, and so long as the deputy was reasonably efficient, no questions were asked. Some players spent the whole of their time deputising in this way, for good theatres liked to have the best players nominally in their service, even though they only came in person occasionally.

The system had obvious abuses, quite apart from its artistic negations. It encouraged the practice of farming-out a whole series of engagements. A well-known player could take four or five engagements for the same day, and distribute them among his friends or pupils, often taking a substantial commission in the process. It was not unusual for one player to be the more or less permanent provider of whatever personnel was needed for a particular combination, and this personnel might be as casual and changeable in detail as the provider found convenient or economical. Under such conditions even the best orchestras were variable and unstable, disciplined rehearsing was impossible, and every performance something of a gamble.

It was not only the rank and file who were infected with this casual attitude. Two conductors were once heard seriously discussing an opera season in which they were to collaborate. Owing to other engagements neither of them was free for the whole of a particular day. They therefore arranged that one of them should take the rehearsal in the morning and the other the performance at night. And when someone protested at this absurdity he was met by the retort: 'Well, it won't be the same band, anyway.'

Billy had many stories of these accidental and undisciplined incidents. To an incompetent deputy an exasperated conductor once shouted: 'I thought you could play the flute.' 'I thought so too,' was the answer. 'I reckon we've both been had!' Another conductor, a visitor, was given an unusual number of rehearsals for a particularly difficult programme, and was in despair at the new faces and changed places which appeared every time the orchestra met. He noticed, however, one faithful soul who had attended every practice, and after the last one he specially thanked him. The reply was: 'Well, sir, that's very good of you, and I'm sorry I shan't be at the concert.' Perhaps Billy's best story of the manners and customs of certain types of player was his description of a drum part on which was scribbled, over a long rest: 'Just time to get a drink, if the barmaid's quick.'

At the same time there was one remarkable result of this happy-go-lucky system, of which the tradition still survives. London orchestral players can read at sight and give competent performances with less preparation than any comparable players in the world. They will attack and master new works with an accuracy, a speed, and a resilience that no foreign players can approach. No other orchestras in the world could play through a London Promenade season and give as many fine performances and make as few mistakes as the good London orchestras will.

And the great continental conductors soon discovered this. Their first visits appeared to them to be rather desperate ventures, with few rehearsals, elusive players, and uneasy discipline. But somehow things went well 'on the night,' and the best of them learnt that if their own technique and personality were sufficiently strong and convincing, they could achieve performances quite as memorable, and in some ways more moving and spontaneous, than the better drilled orchestras of the continent were always able to give. Richter, Nikisch, and Weingartner, to name no others, found the London players very remarkable in their combination of high technical skill, infallible sightreading, and instant response.

It was in this hard school that Billy graduated. It was in competition with the best of these players, and under the eye of these world-renowned conductors, that he became the leader of leaders. In early days he played with every orchestra there was. Later he was permanently identified with the London Symphony. He led it for many of its most famous years, and was its chairman when he died.

The formation of the London Symphony Orchestra was itself an indirect effect of the deputy system, and it is curious to recall now the fact that it was formed because its original members would not forego what they considered their right to employ deputies. Sir Henry Wood was the first firm reformer, and when he insisted, after years of experience, that his famous Queen's Hall Orchestra must accept a new kind of contract, in which deputies were expressly forbidden, many of his leading players left him. These leaders decided to form a new orchestra, the London Symphony, on a co-operative basis, and ruled by a committee of its own members. The orchestra engaged guest conductors, and at its London series of concerts the members played without fee. On the reputation thus gained the orchestra received most of the best provincial engagements and many in the London neighbourhood too. It is still co-operative and ruled from within.

At first the deputy system was tolerated freely, for it was a fundamental condition of the formation. But time was against the practice, and the urge towards permanent and regular membership too strong. By the time the later London Philharmonic and B.B.C. orchestras were founded the London Symphony was also to all intents fixed, both in its personnel and in its organisation. Where it differed from the others was in the absence of a permanent conductor. This made the responsibility and character of the leader of the utmost importance, and Billy became that essential pivot.

He thus covered the whole change of orchestral outlook, so far as internal cohesion and discipline were concerned, while at the same time he worked under a greater variety of conductors, many of them of supreme eminence, than any player ever did before or is likely to do again. Hence Billy's inexhaustible store of anecdote, reminiscence, and the thousand stresses and accidents of private rehearsal and public performance. Hence too his quite authoritative, exact, and almost complete knowledge of every musical tradition of importance. Richter, Nikisch, Steinbach, Weingartner, Mengelberg, Koussevit-sky, and a dozen more of the greatest names, he knew well, not only by isolated concerts, but by many extended tours. And he led for every British conductor, every provincial festival, and nearly every society in the country, at one time or another.

The relationship between the leader of an orchestra and its conductor is in many ways unique. He is in the first place the most important channel of communication. The attitude of an orchestra, its spirit, its readiness, and its loyalty, depend very largely on the demeanour and efficiency of the leaders. And a conductor is really helpless if his leaders either cannot or will not lead. Under the peculiar conditions of the London Symphony it was often the task of the leader, either by word or example, to try and translate into action what an inarticulate or floundering conductor was attempting to say. Foreign conductors sometimes produced incomprehensible or ludicrous English. One of them thought certain players were too jocular and said: 'Jhentlemen, a jhoke, then and now, yess; but always, by Gott, never!' Another wished to hear more of the bass and said: 'Ze baass iz not to hearr. Ze baass iz not to hearr.' And when Billy tried to translate, cut him off with: 'Ssh! don't shpoke.'

On the technical side the leader must be an authority, particularly as regards phrasing and bowing. He is often asked to edit the bowing of all the string parts. Here Billy was a master. He would, if asked, play a phrase in a variety of ways and ask the conductor to choose and adopt whichever seemed most fitting. His experience and skill was always at hand, but never obtruded. A conductor now famous on two continents tells how he was once called upon to conduct one of the Elgar symphonies for the first time at very short notice, and how nervous he felt when he found that Billy was to be his leader. For Billy knew the mind of Elgar as no one else did. This conductor found, however, that though Billy would advise if asked, he would never either parade his knowledge or attempt to force it on anyone. He led firmly as ever, but always with an eye to what the conductor genuinely wished to do, whether it agreed with tradition or not. It was this combination of qualities, authority without ostentation, knowledge without egotism, which made Billy the ideal leader he was.

Temperamental conductors, not to mention superficial and incompetent ones, found Billy a rock on which they could safely lean. If an ignorant or absent-minded conductor made a wild gesture at the wrong time, Billy sat unmoved, ignored the wrong cue, and brought in his section at the right time. There are countless stories of these lapses. One quite famous choral conductor, hearing a bang on the drum which he did not expect, shouted: 'Who did that?' Another, who had great orchestral experience, but trusted his memory far more than it deserved, made a vigorous sign to the drummer with no result. 'Have you nothing to play there?' he asked. 'No, Sir.' 'Well you might do something. You make me look such a fool.'

There used to be a well-known procedure for mildly baiting a conductor who was too fussy. It was called 'opening the shop'. One player would begin by asking a question about his part. Then another, and so on, while the conductor turned backwards and forwards in the score verifying this and arguing that. Ten or fifteen minutes would go by and give the orchestra a welcome rest. But it did not always succeed. It was tried once on a conductor who many years before had been himself an orchestral player. At the first question of this kind he smiled blandly and said: 'Thank you, the shop is shut.' Every orchestral leader tells stories of this kind. Billy had survived more, and remembered more, than anyone else of his time.

Yet he was never cynical, never disparaging, except of pure pretence. And that there can be a good deal of pretence behind a reputation, no one with inside knowledge will deny. There are conductors claiming considerable repute whose ability is superficial, whose ear is uncertain, but who parade an unblushing showmanship which impresses and hoodwinks the audience; so long, that is, and only so long, as the players they are supposed to be directing are clever enough and loyal enough to see that things go well, conductor or no. A fulsome lady once said to a popular conductor: 'How marvellously you follow the band!' There have been many highly applauded performances where that remark would not have been out of place.

The London Symphony Orchestra once played a complicated modern work under three or four famous conductors in succession, all using the same orchestral parts. Yet it was not until still another visitor came, who really knew what every note should be, that a whole series of printed errors were discovered and corrected. Nor are composers any more infallible than conductors. A very distinguished composer was once asked at a rehearsal if a certain note in a succession of chords was G or G sharp. 'Will you play the passage again?' he asked. The orchestra played it. 'That is right' he said, 'the note is G.' 'But I played G sharp!' said the player concerned. The fact is that the accurate hearing of a complex orchestral score demands phenomenal sensitiveness and phenomenal experience. Few men who have not lived in or very near a full orchestra for many years are competent to give a reliable opinion about details. And an orchestra soon discovers whether it is really being accurately heard in detail or not. No gesticulating, showmanship, or temperamental ardour deceives the players. They normally play well, if only for mere pride's sake, for they do not want to take part in a bad performance. But they are often sorely tried.

One sound test of a leader, as of a conductor, is the management, not of experienced professionals, but of average or less-than-average players. Here Billy was indeed a tower of strength, either as a leader or conductor. As a conductor he never aspired to be a star, though he fulfilled many occasional and important engagements with unfailing competence. Time after time he conducted big programmes at an hour's notice, when accident or illness prevented the official conductor from being present. He had played under the greatest. He had helped many of the less endowed. He was at once too humble and too proud to seek the limelight. But for year after year he devoted his time and skill to conducting amateur societies, teaching and inspiring, and filling them with his own keenness and sense of values.

It was this wide range of sympathy, this mingling of high professional skill with genuine understanding of the amateur, which made him for so many years an ideal leader of festivals, either small or great. The London Symphony Orchestra had at one time almost a monopoly of the best provincial festivals, and of these the most permanent and congenial was that of the Three Choirs. The Three Choirs Festival has many virtues. It is annual, it varies its place but not its character, and whether it be at Hereford, Gloucester or Worcester, it is organised, not by a professional conductor who might attend too much to his own tastes or his own personal success, but by a musician who is also a conductor and has strong local attachments and a long and living tradition. Superficial visitors sometimes urge the engagement of some visiting conductor of special repute outside. That will never happen, it is to be hoped, for if it does the Three Choirs will be near its end. If a festival is to be a mere orgy of music, occuring at long intervals and having no permanent roots, then perhaps a distinguished guest-conductor may justify himself. He comes, he plays his part, he goes. He may, or may not, come again. He stimulates a temporary feast, a temporary taste, and no more.

But the Three Choirs is not a temporary feast. The chorus is largely permanent, and works for a good part of the year, and every year. The orchestra is professional and comes from London, but it comes every year and its personnel varies little. The public is largely permanent too, for the local patrons far outnumber those who come from a distance. And it is just this local atmosphere, this local support, that only a local conductor can hold and foster. Many provincial events have been given a temporary brilliance by the importation of a foreign stimulus. Many have thereby lost their local roots and deteriorated into celebrity concerts. The choice is often only too plain. Music can be either a living and indigenous art, or it can be 'an exotic entertainment'. The Three Choirs has always chosen to be the former, and it has 200 years of life behind it.

Moreover, the Three Choirs has been closely associated with native composers, and particularly with Elgar. He was born there, lived and wrote there, and was at home there as nowhere else. He found, as many others have found, that nowhere is there a more genuine

191

care for what is really creative, or a more unselfish desire to do well. This tradition and this spirit have been made and fostered by the three successions of cathedral organists who in turn design and control the festival.

It is clear, however, that in such a festival the permanent leader of the orchestra is in a position of very great influence. All three conductors should find in him the most skilled, helpful and dynamic personality in the whole structure. In Billy they all found precisely that. He could bring his wide experience to the choice of orchestral works and of solo artists. He knew every composer of importance or promise. He had a practical flair for just what could be accomplished with given people in a given time. And it is no more than his due to say that for the whole time of his leadership he was an essential link in every plan, in every performance. He thus held a unique place in the admiration and affection of the Three Choirs organisation, from the three conductors down to the humblest amateur or the smallest choir boy in the chorus.

People often asked Billy what he thought of the great men he had worked with. He was a born conversationalist and story-teller, with most infecting gifts of mimicry and memory. Many are the times he had been urged to write a book about music and musicians from his own unique experiences and vivid recollections. Alas, that book can never now be written, though there are many men who will remember various facets of his talk as long as they live. He was perhaps at his best at the luncheon table of the Royal College of Music, where for many years he taught. At that table he was among intimate friends who had wide knowledge of his own world, and he could speak freely, aptly and generously without too much dotting of i's and crossing of t's. His fund of stories was apparently inexhaustible, and to the day of his death he was constantly recollecting past incidents and illustrations which were new even to those who had sat with him for years.

Many of his stories will be passed on from friend to friend, but none of us can hope to reproduce the verve, the twinkle, the laugh, and the irresistibly convincing imitations of voice and manner with which he told them. Experiences of his own of every kind, grave and gay, flowed from his lips, and particularly his encounters with the more disconcerting incidents of the platform, and the qualities and oddities of conductors and performers ...

192

One conductor perspired so much that he had to change completely in the interval. He came back not as carefully dressed as he might have been. Billy saw the omission, jumped up and held his violin part in front of the conductor, pretending to ask a question, while he said 'Do your buttons up. Do your buttons up.' Four very ample singers once came on and stood in a row in front of Billy's desk, and his neighbour whispered: 'the balloon barrage.' Billy passed this remark on to Rachmaninoff, who was in the artist's room. It was one of the rare occasions on which Rachmaninoff was heard to laugh.

There was a conductor who said to his orchestra: 'Gentlemen, at 12 o'clock Herr So-and-so is coming to play his concerto with us. Remember, gentlemen, that if he hears the orchestra at all while he is playing he will say it is too loud, and we shall be here a long time.' Never were such pianissimos. Another one was rehearsing for the first time a work by Tchaikovsky. The inevitable tune came and he said: 'Quite a nice tune, Billy!' Then it returned. 'What again?' said the conductor, and when it came a third time he stopped the orchestra and said: 'Gentlemen, enough! We must make a cut.' It was of this conductor that the story is told how at the beginning of a tour a certain symphony took forty-five minutes to play, and at the end only fifteen!

There was a whole group of stories about an artist whose financial and matrimonial affairs were in a perpetual tangle. Once a messenger from the lawyers tried to catch him at a rehearsal. He excused himself by saying: 'The Official Receiver wants me. For what he may not be about to receive, may the Lord make him thankful.' On another occasion a new companion was introduced as his wife. 'How changed she is,' said a candid friend. He was something of a counterpart to the famous woman pianist who was announced at a party as being about to play the second movement of the third sonata by her fourth husband. Even better was the gossip writer's paragraph which said that a certain soloist had been married five times, of which the second and fourth were ideally happy!

But of course Billy could be intently serious too. There was a memorable day in 1939 when Leopold Stokowski turned up un-expectedly to lunch at the R.C.M. He found himself opposite Billy and began at once to ask for impressions and details of the great conductors Billy had known. The discussion at one point turned on bowing, and it was interesting to hear Stokowski, whose orchestral discipline is so strict, passionately defending individual freedom of bowing, in all but the most obvious passages. Here Billy wholly agreed with him. No two hands and arms are alike, no two wrists, no two fingers. What is comfortable for one player is impossible or awkward for another. If you want every man in an orchestra to play like an artist, and this was Stokowski's text, you must give him the freedom to do it.

On the subject of the greatest of all the conductors he had known, Billy never wavered. Nikisch was his ideal. Other men were giants too, Richter and Steinbach and Weingartner, but no one of them combined all the gifts as Nikisch did. He was dominant but never domineering. He was effective without a show of it. He was careful without pedantry, supremely endowed without conceit. You played more freely under him than under anyone else, and yet you were conscious of a more perfect and subtle ensemble than any other conductor could achieve. He would sometimes walk to the rostrum in that quiet way of his and then, if the work demanded it, begin with a gesture so sudden and emphatic that every bow leaped to the string and the music was launched with an electrifying attack and vitality. He wasted no beats, and in a quiet contemplative movement would sometimes hardly beat at all. Yet no difficult corner ever came without a look or a sign that was just clear enough to help the players round it. He was kindly, and remarkably economical, in rehearsal, saying just enough, never too much. His influence, like that of all the greatest, was really indirect. He knew every note of every part, and he soon knew the players and made them feel that he knew them, not as fallible or individual men, but as the human instruments of a perfect combination. Every note was in his mind, and all of it was music. There could be no slackness, no shallowness, under such an influence. This is, after all, the secret of all fine conducting, that the conductor should really know the music and then live in it. Then the players will play and live too. It has been said that every orchestra plays as badly as the conductor will let it. It is also said that any professional orchestra will play well if the conductor does not interfere. These two half-truths are a part of the whole truth, of which Nikisch, in Billy's opinion, was the highest example. You played well because, while demanding the utmost co-operation from all, Nikisch yet preserved the individuality of every part.

Nor could there be a more fitting epitaph on Billy himself. Few men knew so much as he did, but no man was ever stifled by him. He trained young players, he trained young conductors. He led great events and small ones, with equal ardour and equal devotion. He is the first and only orchestral player who has been given a Royal decoration and an academic degree for that particular form of service to music. They were well and truly earned. He has been one of the great formative influences of all that is best in a very wide circle of musical endeavour.

(Privately printed in an edition of 100 copies)

Sir Henry Wood

... Sir Henry's whole life was devoted to the faith that the art of music is all one. From whatever nation, or whatever class, the inspiration may come, if it serves the art of music, it is in that noble succession which is above all distinctions of race or creed. Music is the nearest approach to a universal language that our civilisation has yet achieved. In that universal language, and for that wide civilisation, Sir Henry worked.

The annual series of Promenade Concerts, which he made into a national institution, was unique in its range. He developed those programmes until they became a veritable National Gallery of all the finest music that exists. At no other time in history, and at no other place in the world, has it been possible for the music lover to hear so much good music so faithfully presented. Sir Henry achieved this by virtue of two gifts, both outstanding and both essential. He had a mind broad enough to be sympathetic to all schools, and he had a method so conscientious and so versatile, that nothing was either too small or too great for his ears and attention.

I will give you two of my own experiences of these qualities. Many years ago I was one of those young composers, and there have been hundreds of us in all, who were given a hearing by Sir Henry. He asked me to come and see him, and he gave me then and there nearly an hour of his time while I played through my work and he asked questions and made notes about it.

On another occasion, when I was organising concerts in Winchester, I asked Sir Henry to come and conduct our local orchestra,

195

and I suggested a Symphony then rarely played. He replied that he had conducted over 4,000 works, but not that one, and he would be delighted to do it. Moreover, he sent us a complete set of parts, with his own careful markings, and I heard afterwards that he had even found a chance of rehearsing it privately elsewhere, before he came to us to conduct it in public.

The number of private rehearsals at the piano which he gave to soloists, and particularly young soloists, was beyond count. He would never waste the time of an orchestral rehearsal by discussing points that could be agreed at the piano beforehand. And all those who came to him, either for audition or for preliminary consultation, were given a fine lesson in patience, attention and care for detail.

These were qualities that made his achievements possible, and they were bestowed with unwavering fidelity for half a century. Whether you were a young student making a first appearance, or an artist of international repute, made no difference. You got your fair share of Sir Henry's time, ability and resources. Indeed the established artist was far more likely to exhaust his patience than the nervous youngster, just as he was naturally more exacting when dealing with a professional orchestra than when training amateurs or students.

And he had many accomplishments outside music, vast as his musical work was. He was well-read, he was a talented painter and a fine craftsman. He ordered his life as he ordered his concerts, punctual, unhasting, unwasting. We therefore remember again today, and shall long remember, with pride and gratitude, that life of great accomplishment, that loyalty and devotion, that broad humanity.

(Introduction to the Henry Wood Memorial Concert,
March 4 1945)

Envoi – Festival of Britain

There are many ways in which it is possible to consider a nation's music. Do we mean our history – what has been accomplished in the past, and what was our contribution to the general musical heritage of the world? Or do we mean our repute today, as composers, or conductors, or specialized performers? Or do we mean the interest and work of the enormous amateur body of music-lovers and music-makers, which is the background of our musical endeavour? The musical rank of a nation may vary greatly when viewed from these several standpoints separately.

Historically, for example, our greatest period was between three and four centuries ago, and it is only comparatively recently that we, and some of our foreign friends, have begun to realize how great that period was. The revival and rediscovery of Tudor music has been an outstanding feature of the last fifty years, and we can claim without fear of contradiction that Tallis, Byrd, Gibbons, Dowland and their many contemporaries were comparable in musical rank and achievement to the writers of the triumphant Tudor era of poetry and drama which has long been universally accepted as one of the richest periods in the world's literature.

We are also rediscovering Purcell; but there is no doubt that Purcell's century, the seventeenth, and still more its successor, the eighteenth, did not produce in England anything approaching the contemporary developments of music elsewhere, first in Italy, and later in Germany. The ascendancy of Italy is strikingly shown in all those musical terms which are the common language of music. The eminence of Germany still fills our programmes with the names of Bach, Haydn, Mozart, Beethoven, Schubert, Schumann, Brahms and Wagner, who between them cover the two centuries preceding our own. Even if we call Handel half an Englishman, he was German by birth and retained also many features of the Italian tradition. Only in his later period of devotion to oratorio have we any substantial share in his fame.

It is primarily this dearth of English names in the musical history of

197

the two centuries between 1700 and 1900 which has made the world think of us, until quite recently, as a people without serious musical traditions.

Similarly, on the executive and performing side, for one English name in this same period there are a hundred Italian, French and German names still recorded and remembered. It was the Italians who invented opera, and with it the whole tradition of operatic singing. France followed Italy, but added little more than a French flavour to what was predominantly Italian in origin. It was Germany that produced the sublime sacred music, first of Schutz and finally of Bach, than which nothing greater has ever been achieved. And it was also Germany which evolved those great and basic conceptions of instrumental music, sonata, quartet and symphony, which are, as it were, the grammar, logic, and architecture of the myriad examples of pure music which Western civilization has since created and enjoyed.

Only towards the very end of the nineteenth century did this Italian and German ascendancy begin to find competition elsewhere. Russia in particular found sources of inspiration of its own; so to a very appreciable extent did Spain, and last, but by no means least, arose some clear indications of an English renaissance, a renaissance which has now placed us in the front rank again. We are today well able to measure ourselves, from this creative point of view, against the best that our contemporary world can show.

Our music, considered thus historically, and from the specialized creative angle, is a chequered chronicle, with some highlights, but many long and blank spaces. And if this were the whole story, we should have to be content with modest claims, reserving our pride for the two isolated periods — that of today, and the other of some three hundred and fifty years ago, with Purcell as a lonely genius near the end of the seventeenth century.

But this is by no means the whole story, for it takes little account of the extent to which music may be a permanent and spontaneous feature in the life of the ordinary citizen, whose talent may not be highly specialized, but who, in the social and corporate activities which are his chosen forms of civilization, may devote himself with fair skill to all the arts or crafts which appeal to him naturally and directly. Of these music is one, and though such spontaneous and communal singing or playing may have no particular claim to fame, it may well be as much and as real a part of the social fabric as any other fruit of the human mind and heart.

It is from this social angle that the story of music in Britain is most satisfying and illuminating, for nowhere else in the world have men and women more freely and consistently combined to produce concerted amateur music of all kinds. There have been few, even of the smaller villages, without a choir of some kind, and few of even the smaller towns without a group of players. And our larger amateur societies are without parallel, either in numbers or quality, anywhere else in the world.

Many causes have combined to produce this spontaneous habit of concerted music which has been so marked a feature of our social life. Of these causes there are two that deserve special mention. The first is a fundamentally democratic attitude towards corporate activities of all kinds. We have never for long been governed and regimented from above. The springs of our civic life have been for many centuries fed from the ordinary levels of citizenship. Our parish councils, municipal corporations, groups, unions and committees of all kinds have accustomed us to think of all the major activities of social life essentially as teamwork. This was true even in the isolated agricultural communities of the later Middle Ages. The industrialism of workshop and factory, bringing men into ever closer and more concentrated relations, merely accentuated this group-feeling, and there is hardly a single social movement, from a football club to a national political party, which has not begun with a committee of like-minded individuals, drawn from any or from all classes of the population, and this committee habit is retained and strengthened as the movement grows. A church, a chapel, or a club organizes a choir, a mine or a factory will create a brass band, a school or college will form a modest orchestra. These are at once the basis and the strength of our most active musical traditions.

The second cause which has made our musical life in some respects unique, and in every major respect social and national, is the fact that in England the Protestant Reformation did not destroy the musical traditions of the Established Church. It changed the language of religion from Latin to English, but it retained the art of music in religious worship virtually unaltered. Every student of history knows that the music of Western Europe, which is the common heritage of us all, was created in the medieval church. Singing in parts, which gave us the whole fundamental structure of our harmony, was developed and perfected in the cathedrals and monasteries of the Middle Ages. The Latin motet and canticle, which was the musical origin of the secular madrigal or part-song, which was in turn the foundation on which concerted instrumental music was first built, was a product of the church, and this musical tradition has never been broken in England. Our people therefore had these models constantly in their ears, and when they made music for themselves they could not do other than copy that music and that method which had adorned their corporate worship from time immemorial.

It was the same tradition which brought music into our schools, to an extent which surpasses any other national system of education. The monastic schools had taught the music of the liturgy. The secular schools therefore accepted music as a natural and inevitable part of a broad education, and there is an unbroken chain of musical activity stretching from the choir schools of five hundred years ago down to the singing-classes in our primary schools today. Nowhere else in the world is there so much school music or so large a repertory of music written for school use. It is these children who ultimately feed our choral and orchestral societies and provide our democratic audiences. This is the essential background of our national music, and though we also have our own share of musicians who are highly gifted and specialized, these are not a class apart to the same extent as may happen in countries where active participation in music is not so widespread.

In many continental countries music was for long periods mainly the concern of the royal court or the noble household, rather than of the ordinary citizen. The tendency then was to concentrate attention on the specially gifted, and to encourage those forms of music which only the exceptional artist could adequately perform. Opera is a clear case of this kind. It owed its origin and development to munificent patronage; it sought, trained and supported the few who were specially gifted; and it invited discrimination and taste, but not necessarily any active knowledge or participation, outside the specialized circle. Oratorio, as we know it in Britain, is an example of a different approach, and one more in consonance with our own desires. We want not only to be musical, but to be actively so, and we therefore amass huge choruses and contrive also to include large numbers of amateur orchestral players, so that the performance shall be that of a community, rather than a purely specialized and selective effort. It would be foolish to condemn either attitude. There is room in the world for both. What we need to keep clear in our minds are the varied purposes and approaches that exist in the world of music as a whole, each one answering and fulfilling some genuine and spontaneous instinct towards artistic progress and expression.

The story of our music thus differs fundamentally from that of Italy or France or Germany, because there has never been in England that consistent patronage of music by kings or governments which was almost the universal feature of the courts, large or small, and of many of the more opulent cities of Europe. After the flowering of the Tudor period we have only one master of world-wide repute to boast of — Henry Purcell — until we come to the present day. And even Purcell was never able to achieve what he might have done had he commanded the resources of some of his foreign contemporaries. Meanwhile Italy, France and Germany were producing the singers, the players and the composers whose names and achievements are now the common heritage of us all, and England was chiefly known as a place where foreign music and musicians could find a warm and lucrative welcome. The only permanent native tradition which continued its modest and unbroken sequence was that of the churches, the schools, and the amateur groups of all kinds which never ceased to feed themselves and practise the music that best suited them. The more elaborate ventures of the theatre or concert-hall relied mainly on imported music, or on music which imitated an imported fashion.

Handel came to us, and in the field of oratorio became virtually one of us, for he provided those masterpieces of cantata and oratorio which so exactly agreed with our resources and temperament. He dominated the eighteenth century. In the nineteenth, Spohr and Mendelssohn were welcomed with almost equal fervour, and by about 1850 the prestige of Mendelssohn dwarfed every English name and provided the standard by which every native effort was judged. We played, of course, the sonatas, quartets and symphonies of Haydn, Mozart and Beethoven, and we were among the first to sing the works of Bach, then being rediscovered after the neglect of a whole century. We welcomed in turn the music of Schubert, of Schumann, of Wagner, Berlioz and Brahms, but until about 1880 there was no specifically British music that could pretend to rank, either at home or abroad, with what Europe had produced and was still producing. We performed most of these masterpieces, but we did not create them.

At long last, however, there arose a group of young men, of whom Arthur Sullivan, Alexander Mackenzie, Hubert Parry and Charles Stanford were the chief, who by their work and influence gradually changed the whole perspective of music in Britain, and laid the foundations of that creative renaissance which has now brought us into the front rank of musical nations, both as composers and executants. Sullivan's comic operas, Mackenzie's orchestral skill, Parry's choral works and Stanford's astonishing versatility, all of them showing a personal and native flavour, began to challenge the foreign ascendancy, and although none of them reached the secure fame of a world-wide repute, they were shortly joined by a fifth name, that of Edward Elgar, which did. To these should be added the somewhat lonely but exceptionally sensitive genius of Frederick Delius, and we then have a fair picture of the creative promise with which we were able to face the world when the twentieth century began.

During the fifty years of the immediate past we need fear no comparison from any quarter whatever. Of the three or four greatest names in contemporary music that of Vaughan Williams is certainly one. Gustav Holst, Arnold Bax, Frank Bridge, John Ireland and Arthur Bliss have each added to the body of British music acknowledged everywhere, and in William Walton we have a composer whose every work has been an event of major importance. Youngest of all, and astonishingly successful, is Benjamin Britten, who meets on equal terms the leaders in that field of opera which has hitherto been considered outside the range of the English composer.

It is significant that nearly all these contemporary composers, and the same is true of many of our leading performers, were pupils of the two chief schools of music, the Royal Academy and the Royal College. It was Mackenzie who vitalized the Royal Academy, and Parry and Stanford who developed the Royal College. The number and calibre of Stanford's pupils is especially remarkable, and many more well-known names belong to his group. The Royal Manchester College, closely linked with the famous Hallé Orchestra, has also contributed substantially to our present quality, and the recent organization of the Royal Scottish Academy promises to add a further share.

202

Two new influences have added greatly to the range and appreciation of music in this century. The first was the invention of the gramophone, which enabled the music-lover to hear and study the better-known masterpieces in a way that was not possible merely by listening to isolated performances in the concert-hall. Then came wireless broadcasting, which basically changed the musical world. Its effects were not all gain, for incessant broadcasting may spoil the taste of listeners, and much of what is broadcast is of a shallow and ephemeral nature. But broadcasting also includes the best, and it has awakened in numberless listeners, who would not otherwise have come into touch with the best music at all, a permanent and satisfying appreciation of the better programmes. Broadcasting also adds enormously to the repute, and incidentally to the material prosperity, of the composers and performers which it favours, and there is ample evidence that a great many listeners are led by this experience of broadcasting to seek the more direct contacts of public concerts and recitals heard at first hand.

Up to this point all our music had been the fruit of private enterprise, the spontaneous devotion, skill and generosity of countless musicians and music-lovers. The final reward of direct help from the State came very late, and as so often happens in our social history, by circumstances which were in the first place improvised to meet an emergency. The second World War temporarily destroyed the whole field of public music-making. It was quickly realized that this was a social catastrophe, not only for the musicians, but for the very large public for whom music was a relaxation, a recreation or a stimulus. The idea gained ground that if the audience could not reach its music, then the music must be taken to the audience. This was the genesis of the factory concerts, of the groups of artists, large and small, who were encouraged to visit towns and villages and give the hard-pressed war-workers, troops in training, evacuated men, women and children, and indeed any kind of audience that could be found anywhere, a chance to hear that music which could not be organized in the normal fashion of peace-time. These concerts were subsidized in the first place by the Carnegie and Pilgrim Trusts, but the Treasury quickly added to these resources and ultimately took complete financial responsibility.

Thus arose the Arts Council of Great Britain, which is now a State enterprise supported by public funds, and exists to foster and maintain all the arts. It has enabled Covent Garden to be reopened as a permanent Opera House. It has put those two unique organizations, the Old Vic and Sadler's Wells, beyond fear of collapse through lack of means, it has helped the chief professional orchestras, and it keeps a watchful and sympathetic eye on artistic ventures of all kinds. Late in the day, but very effectively and appropriately, we have inaugurated that public patronage of the arts which many of our Continental neighbours have so long enjoyed. And it is impossible to exaggerate the benefits that may accrue to all the arts, and to the taste and enlightenment of our whole people, if these new resources are consistently and wisely used.

This, then, is the present state of our music. We have two permanent opera houses producing not only a range of classics but offering also new and native works to which the whole world pays attention. We have half-a-dozen professional orchestras of high rank offering programmes second to none in breadth and quality. We have indeed in the London Promenade Concerts an orchestral feast without parallel, either in the wealth of its programmes or the size of its audiences. Fifty years ago the genius and energy of Sir Henry Wood inaugurated this series, which, under his unremitting skill and devotion, became a very remarkable feature of our musical life. We have amateur societies and groups beyond number, covering choral, orchestral and chamber music of all kinds, not to mention those more popular brass and military bands which do so much to enliven the leisure hours both of their players and supporters. We have our great cathedral, our church and chapel choirs which continue to uphold the standards of sacred music. We have the large provincial festivals, among which that of the Three Choirs has the longest and finest history of any comparable organization in the world. And we have composers, conductors and performers of international rank and fame, and of conspicuous breadth of view.

Above all, we have an educational system which finds room for music from the nursery school to the University. It is now virtually impossible for any really outstanding talent to remain undiscovered; and our Local Education Authorities have the means and the power to see that such talents are not lost for lack of help, either by instruction or subsidy. Our Royal and other Schools of Music have the apparatus, the staffs, and the scholarships with which to give a highly specialized training. Our Universities have flourishing musical faculties, and there thus exists a complete ladder for the specially gifted to climb. All these things foster and enhance the public interest in music, and this is the most important consideration of all. For a nation is only truly and genuinely musical when taste and discrimination permeates every section of the people. Moreover, the arts are at their best when men not only encourage them, but actively pursue them to the limit of their own powers, be they small or great. Viewed thus broadly, our prospects are full of hope. We have a fruitful past, an active present, and the promise of a solid and creative future.

(From the Symposium *Our Way of Life*, 1951)